The Power to Bless

The Power to Bless

MYRON C. MADDEN

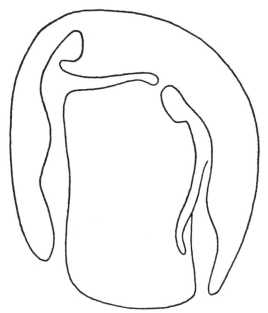

🔶 ABINGDON PRESS

NASHVILLE—NEW YORK

A father should bring blessing to his children, not seek his children to bless him. To that end, I speak blessing to five wonderful children who have been a dynamic laboratory in living—

Myron C., Jr.
Julia Anne
John Geren
Benjamin Eldred
Merritt Gray

Preface

The greatest power in primitive religion is the power of "curse." This power remains with us as we listen to it in children, as we hear it in riots and campus disorders, and as we sample the debates of the United Nations. Man seems to look for some high place of office, influence, or notoriety from which he can hurl the destructive word upon his enemy.

The new thing in religion came with Abraham—the "blessing" and the intent of God to bring blessing upon all the families of the earth. This is a power stronger than the power of curse, and it orders life around the new concept of God as the one who gives blessing instead of a "blessing out."

The heart of the gospel is bound up in the fact that God drew man's outrage and curse upon himself without cursing back. Instead of curse, there was a return of blessing. This is the new initiative of God to rob man's invective of its poisonous power to destroy his brother. It takes away man's right to damn another in God's name or power while it gives him the high privilege to bless in the name of God.

Modern psychology has contributed much to our understanding of life under curse. One of its goals is that of removing the stigma, stain, or feelings of isolation and rejection that tend to prevent wholesome relationships and meaningful living. It is my conviction that the psychiatrist, the medical doctor, and the psychologist need the authority of the gospel behind their efforts. Their many words could be fortified by one word—the word of blessing. I am not advocating that they take on the priestly role in addition to their professional roles, but I suggest that their work of bringing men to health and wholeness can be greatly helped by the good word of God's acceptance coming from a trusted man of faith. We need to work together!

The word of the Scripture needs to be represented in a person who takes godly initiative to speak the deep word of forgiveness and acceptance. The man who can do this is a healer of the highest order because he removes the deepest malady, the inner feeling of curse and condemnation. The man who brings the word of blessing needs to know that he must speak it through the resistance of the child in each person. The "child within" tends to nurture all his past curses and abuses. If he does not get them out in a purging and cleansing, they tend to go to his children and his community no matter how hard he consciously tries to overcome them.

Several years ago I read an article by a close personal friend, Dr. Karl A. Olsson, in which he characterized Christians as "the people of the blessing." From that article and idea has come much of what is written here. I must also give him credit for his patience and encouragement in following what I have written.

Dr. Wayne E. Oates, my professor and trusted friend, has been a real blessing in going through the material of the manuscript line upon line. He has made suggestions that actually called for much rewriting and focusing of the material to the concerns of Christian people generally rather than to pastors only.

My friends in the Institute of Religion and Health of Louisiana, Inc. are due a special word of appreciation, and particularly Dr. T. A. Watters, psychoanalyst, whose insights have shown that "blessing" and "curse" are a vivid reality in the lives of all people. A word of thanks goes to my students in Clinical Pastoral Education over the past nine years at Southern Baptist Hospital, along with the Administration, as together we have sought to make an effective alliance of medicine with religion in the healing community of the hospital.

These pages could not have been written without the fortification of those persons whose lives were open in trust and meaningful response in counseling. They and still others have taught me much of the joy of being alive in the fullest sense of the word—the relationship of giving and receiving blessing.

A special and endearing word of blessing goes to my wife, Mary Ben, who has often gone unblessed while this manuscript was wrought out.

Contents

Section 1

THE NATURE OF THE VOW
AND THE CURSE

Section 2

THE POWERS OF BLESSING
AND HEALING

Section 1

THE NATURE OF THE VOW AND THE CURSE

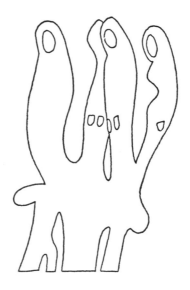

I

The Child in the Man—the Vow

Modern man finds himself in need of resources
that will bestow wholeness and oneness. Meaningful religion speaks of rebirth and bringing man to a
state of blessing. In order to come to blessing man
needs to be free from the feeling of "curse." If religion accomplishes its aim it must have the energy
and strength to give more than "positive thinking."
The pastor or the man of religious faith should be
able to bring positive feeling that can counteract
negative feeling and a sense of personal damnation
or doom.

Primitive religions for the most part focused on
the power to bring curse. Their effectiveness resided
in their ability to control men by the threat of curse

and taboo. Modern religion has not completely gotten away from primitive religion on this point. We have not learned how to bring our children through the preschool years without subjecting them to uncommon fears. Even if we greatly improved our skills it remains doubtful if it is possible for children to go through the early years without personally cursing much of their feeling life, even to the point of denying its presence. Rational man is by nature a threat to the primitive feelings, and vice versa. The child operates almost completely at the feeling level and must deal with parents who have graduated to the rational level, or, at least, who put demands on the child to live by reason.

The child invariably represents threat to the parent because he stands as a constant and living illustration of what the parent has denied in himself. He fears that the child will become a testimony against his own demons of the past. He then reverts to a fearful or angry control of his child in order to keep his own past under better guard. Naturally the child tends to take advantage of the parent's fears so that he may have some bargaining power in a world where he is only a midget in a battle with the giants. For example, a four-year-old boy drops his pants and walks into the living room where his mother is entertaining the missionary circle. Great consternation and confusion follow. In the wake of it all the child discovers powers he did not know he

16

had! Thereafter, he promises not to repeat the action if he is given certain considerations. An anxious mother might even go so far as to let him reign as king in private if only he will allow her a better image in public along with freedom from such painful exposure.

Modern dynamic psychology has helped much in our understanding of the way pastors appreciate the need for a blessing (acceptance) and the fear of a curse (rejection) in themselves and those to whom they minister. It has helped us to understand that culture, education, and sophistication tend to separate a man from the flow of childhood feelings. But it has established positive evidence that the material of primitive man is still brought to modern man in the childhood years. The child is given the task of forgetting much of his strong feeling life as he tries to become a more rational human being.

Where the denial of feelings makes the child assume he cannot be loved with these feelings, he attempts to banish them from memory. But they always pose the problem of his own banishment from love if they come to light. Every man possesses much of the unknown in the shadow side of the self. In childhood it was necessary to thrust many thoughts and feelings aside in order to cope. But such an act does not mean that this vital past of a man is completely cut off from him; it is more accurate to say it is buried alive.

17

THE SPIRITS IN PRISON

If a man were to lose all contact with his childhood memories and feelings, he would indeed be lost. This would take away his choice tastes, his "soul" food, most of his music, half his poetry, as well as the bliss of the holidays and the pleasant feelings around the change of the seasons. Of course it would take away much of his anxiety, guilt feelings, fears of inadequacy, and his battles with a judgmental conscience. We are constantly being rewarded by the goodness and threatened by the fears of childhood.

Most adults carry both pain and blessing from childhood. If the pain is too great it is "energetically barred from becoming conscious." [1] Sometimes this is the only way an adult can manage these sleeping powers. The man who denies his childhood is not rid of it. The material resides as a kind of living mass in his deeper self. If he is able to find relationships of love, trust, and acceptance, these powers of the past tend to lose their ability to haunt and terrify the man of the present.

The man with phobias, fears, depression, deep anxiety, or dreadful guilt will be, in most instances, struggling with some of the pains of his early years. Not all the pain comes from the past. The pains of

[1] Charles Brenner, *An Elementary Textbook of Psychoanalysis* (New York: International Universities Press, 1966), p. 37.

the present can usually be managed in the present. But a person's loss of control is more likely to come when present fears are coupled with "horrible imaginings"—when past and present join in an assault on the self.

The point is that the child still lives in and motivates the man. But the man needs to be able to redirect the energies to more acceptable goals. Dr. W. Hugh Missildine makes this point rather well:

> The "child of the past" actually continues, with all his feelings and his attitudes, to the very end of our lives. *While these feelings may seem undesirable and unreasonable to you as an adult, they are not at all unreasonable in a child—specifically your "child of the past" and the emotional atmosphere in which he lived.*[2]

This is why a man does things that are unreasonable in his own eyes. A man will often go against reason simply because the child within has first call on his energies. This is especially true of the man who has little insight into his "child of the past."

THE VOWS OF CHILDHOOD

One might better understand people by asking what they want, by seeking to know what they are driving after, living for, or demanding of life.

[2] Missildine, *Your Inner Child of the Past* (New York: Simon and Schuster, 1963), p. 25.

This question can never be answered apart from the *vows* of early childhood. No person comes to adult years without a number of such vows. They are the deep commitments that the child makes, relative to growing up and solving frustrations.

The vow is what the child promises himself he will *do* once he is in a stronger position. He thinks about that day when he will be affluent. He impulsively decides right away that much of his income will go toward helping his parents. After hearing them argue over how a few dollars will be spent, he tells himself that when he gets big and prosperous they will be "poor no more." They will never need to fight over money again. He may or may not keep the vow and meet that particular need. That is another story.

The child, before he enters the first grade, has already taken vows about where he will spend at least three fortunes. He is committed for more than he will make the rest of his life.

The same principles apply to the vows of love. A child is a born mediator. He is often terrified by the conflicts of others, especially those of parents and older brothers and sisters. He vows that he will master these conflicts with his love. He promises to love Mother so that she will never have to cry again. If she is widowed or separated, he tries to comfort her. If he fails (as he usually does) he blames his

20

failure on his size and vows to be taken more seriously when he grows up.

Most men and women do not know who this child of the past really is. Or, at least, they do not know themselves in terms of these past vows. The vows are usually made, but are forgotten because later they would seem ridiculous or stupid. But just the fact that they must be submerged means that they are active down inside. In some subtle form, they continue to hold sway.

These vows are an essential part of the defenses people build against getting hurt. It is usually the child who gets hurt most. He is more sensitive to pain and the most open to it. This pain can be physical or emotional. The child trusts more and depends more. As he begins to suffer from the hurts in relation to others, he starts building up a system of protection. He sets up his fortifications against these hurts: they include every form of pain.

The pastor's ministry is not one of determining the origin of every adult motivation. It is, however, necessary that a pastor or any helping person keep in mind that the child in each man is still peeping through every crevice, speaking from every side, and tugging at every step. One person is more understanding of another when he is able to accept that the childhood past can create all manner of disturbance in adult life. With this knowledge, the listener can hear to the depths without getting uneasy.

21

When a pastor listens to an adult, he needs to be able to hear the voice of the child. Then he must ask what it is the child in the man is seeking. The pastor or any other helping person has a right to keep this question in mind at all times. It will serve him well in his understanding of the needs of the other. Then it will make him much more sympathetic and accepting of behavior that is otherwise quite out of the ordinary.

Any pastor who can communicate with the irrational and long-buried material of childhood will be moving toward the central theme of Christianity. Our task is not to destroy nor bury more deeply this childhood material. Rather it is that of helping each person to "become a child again." Perhaps we should add that the direction is twofold: back to childhood and forward to maturity, both in the same movement.

SIGNIFICANCE OF THE VOWS

It is not as easy as it may seem to "put away childish things." Once a vow is made—and forgotten—it tends to get itself performed and fulfilled. This is most "unreasonable." In other words the hidden vow works against all reason. Much of our unreasonable behavior is done to accomplish these stubborn patterns fixed in the first years of life. For instance, a man of thirty-five could never seem to get enough to eat. He lived in constant fear of starvation and this against all reason. He so distrusted his wife to feed him that he would stop on the way home in the evenings to get a hamburger. It happened that he was almost starved as a child and suffered from severe malnutrition. This was in the days before he could consciously remember. His aunt reported it to him years later. Without being aware of it, he was striving to reassure himself that he would not be left hungry again.

We are saying that the "vow" is more than that which is spoken. The old saying expresses it: "The burned child fears the fire." The concept includes emotional conditioning against any form of hurt. A child loses a dog and has a difficult time loving the next dog. If the family loses several pets, he becomes less and less capable of investing his feelings in them. Pastors and parents need to know the importance of interpreting loss and death even when a child is young. A child can do an amazing amount of assimilation with a little help.

If ridicule and scorn are heaped upon a child, he sets himself against such for later years. In fact, ridicule is so painful to a child that he will let his barriers down in many other areas in order to keep this defense strong. He may tend to put all his efforts at self-protection in one single area. This could set him up for a lot of shadowboxing. He will fight at the least hint that someone is about to touch the old scar tissue. He may defend himself in ways other than fighting. He may even invite jokes on himself or tell them about himself so he can control the laughing better. He may resort to running before any attack is begun. Each person adopts his own set of mechanisms. No two are alike.

PHYSICAL FACTORS IN THE VOWS

The better evidences of the "ridicule" factor are seen in people who have some type of deformity or unusual physical characteristic. This is illustrated in the hunchback, the dwarf, or a Richard III. Søren Kierkegaard was such a victim. He said of himself: "Like the kangaroo, I have very short forelegs, and tremendously long hind legs. Ordinarily I sit quite still; but if I move, the tremendous leap that follows strikes terror to all my acquaintances, friends and relatives." [3] No doubt many of the world's great people have had handicaps against which they both labored and suffered.

For the day by day relationships to others, special attention needs to be given to these areas. A certain man who was five feet and three inches

[3] Kierkegaard, *Either/Or*, trans. David F. Swenson and Lillian Marvin Swenson (Princeton: Princeton University Press, 1946), I, 30.

tall always ended his public prayer with "forgive us our shortcomings." He dealt with other men by trying to "cut them down to size." By that he meant down to his size. This particular man had a pastor who understood him and accepted him as he was. At the same time that he took him seriously, he let him know that the life and fellowship of the church would not tolerate his self-proclaimed freedom to attack and cut down at will. The man found greater security. No minister before had faced him honestly and challenged this license. In a real sense he lost with each of the other pastors because they retreated as he set about to cut them down. He desperately needed a pastor who could draw some limits for him, not one who would accommodate him out of fear. At the same time he needed someone who could love him in his anger.

We return to give more attention to the manifestation of the physical factors in these childhood vows. This has much to do with shaping attitudes toward the self. We even ask people what "shape" they are in. Perhaps a quotation from Richard III would be in order to establish how important these scars of scorn can be in an adult. Richard was deformed and came, no doubt, to manhood bearing all the marks of continuous abuse and ridicule. We listen to Shakespeare giving him words:

25

I, that am curtail'd of this fair proportion,
Cheated of feature by dissembling nature,
Deform'd, unfinish'd, sent before my time
Into this breathing world, scarce half made up,
And that so lamely and unfashionable
That dogs bark at me, as I halt by them; . . .
And therefore, since I cannot prove a lover, . . .
I am determined to prove a villain,
And hate the idle pleasures of these days.

(Act I, Scene I)

The pastor may deal with the "villain" without being aware of the causes. The community and church tend to look upon certain people as being black sheep. They do not often have any explanation of background factors. Many of them are hidden except in the most obvious cases, such as the hunchback, the polio victim, and the dwarf.

There are many physical problems children have that mar or damage their self-esteem. Many of these will persist as deep problems in the adult, but may not any longer be obvious. For instance a man may have good physical proportion and still be carrying scars from earlier days when everyone laughed at him as a "fatso." The teeth might have been an earlier focal point of embarrassment. Later dental work can correct the teeth. But it simply has little power to remove the defensive sensitivity to any later laughter.

Another significant problem is that of a sense

of shame regarding shortness of stature, especially in a boy. He may be one of those teen-agers whose growth spurt was rather late, say around sixteen. When this happens, the marks are usually set deeply, no matter how tall he might become in the late teens.

Perhaps one of the most troublesome problems of the teen years is that of acne. This usually leaves very few damaging marks on the skin. But they are plentiful in the spirit. Other physical problems can leave their telling results. They can include birth marks or disfiguring accidents in which the face is cut or the nose broken. Severe ugliness or unusual size of the extremities, such as hands and feet, can create a problem. An early loss of hair for a man or late development of breasts for a woman can be factors worthy of note.

BEYOND THE PHYSICAL FACTORS

A person does not necessarily have to have a grotesque or unusual physical mark to live in dread of ridicule or scorn. Alfred Adler had much to contribute at this point. It is out of these childhood years that the person comes to adulthood with what Adler called "inferiority feelings." One may be physically complete, but still come out of childhood with inner scars. These scars produce guilt and inadequacy. In fact, they mostly come out of feelings of guilt and inadequacy from childhood experience. The child lives as a midget among giants. He needs to overcome this helpless posture. He cannot equalize things if he keeps the ethic imposed on him by adults. That ethic tells him he cannot express his murderous thoughts and feelings. Yet he gets frustrated and comes up with such feelings. He assumes he has tasted the forbidden fruit (do not touch it lest you die!). He feels terrible guilt at breaking the parental commandment. He must hide himself from the eye of the gods. He finds it necessary to conceal most of his thoughts and feelings in order to obtain love and acceptance. In other words, his thoughts must be "covered." When the child hears the footsteps of the giants, he needs some psychological clothing to cover his imagined nakedness. The result is deep denial of his feelings and thoughts; with this goes the feeling of inner curse.

This covering or banishing unacceptable feelings and thoughts leaves its problems. Because of such feelings, a child may judge himself to be unworthy of the love and affection he needs from parents and others. He could tell himself that they love him only because they do not know the whole truth about him. In telling himself he is unworthy of love, he may act in such a way that he gets the amount he feels he deserves. His actions may go to the extreme of defying adults or in some way frustrating their intent to give love. If he is unable to let love cast out his fears, the child can become pixie, charmer, or even clown. He can parade in the vestments of wit and humor and conceal his curse by cutting capers.

TRIANGLE LIVING WITHIN THE FAMILY

One of the greatest problems of the childhood experience is that of the child being allowed to get away with gross manipulation. For example, the bond between husband and wife may be so unsteady that the child will get power over his parents by becoming the balance of power. This can be the start of "using" rather than "caring." Brothers use brothers, sisters use sisters, brothers use sisters, and parents use and are used. Family triangles begin when one person uses another to strengthen himself in relation to the third. A son learns if he sides with his mother he can have his wishes met. A daughter may do the same in relation to her father. A father may listen to his daughter while turning a deaf ear toward his wife. All would go well, but she cannot handle her guilt over having strength her mother does not have. It is not uncommon for a despairing wife to use her more influential daughter to motivate her husband. She will say to the daughter, "Why don't you tell your father we want to go to Mexico on vacation? He will listen to you." It is not altogether uncommon for a son to receive the major share of affection and tenderness from his mother. The father might at the same time find himself a very poor second by comparison.

Children help establish these family triangles, but they want desperately to get out of them. However, these patterns seldom change very much, once they start. The child loves the power he has as a result, but he simply cannot manage his guilt. The guilt arises over what he imagines he has done to the family structure. The boy, for instance, is seldom aware that his father may be too weak to establish his authority as head of the house. Instead the child may feel that by his own power or stealth he has eroded family solidarity.

The child may deplore a weak father under such circumstances and make resolves to be a strong father when he marries. The sad story is that he is usually unable to break the cycle. He tends to repeat it in his son as the son relates to a wife along the same pattern of the past. Not being able to manage the stormy emotions of a woman, he retreats and leaves her to seek consolation and tenderness from her son. This sick state of affairs can go from father to son to the third and fourth generation. Thus the curse can become a shadow over an entire family.

THE CURSE AND THE VOW

The goodwill and positive intent on the part of parents as they help children through the early years is often taken for granted. Actually this is not always the case. Under some circumstances the child comes to feel he has the ill will of one or both parents. He may come to this assumption for many reasons. For one thing, it can come from a factual situation such as the triangle mentioned above. The child in question could be favored by a grandparent in such a way as to bring rejection from one of the parents. He could be an unusually ugly child and get parental rejection. Again he could inherit a position in a family that tends to reject that position. The stepson often falls heir to such rejection. From these and other causes, a child might assume that his family, or some part of it, is hostile toward him. As a preschool child, one is not able to measure the degree of hostility. One simply may feel he has to remain on guard lest he be destroyed. He may take it literally when his father tells him he will "knock his head off."

It is not uncommon for a young child to blame parents when a sibling or a pet dies. A milder reaction to hostile feelings is the thought that perhaps one is an adopted child. This says there is frustration and a feeling of unreality and doubt about the relationship.

31

These strong feelings can result in a child's fearing that he has caused a kind of parental curse. This may be more what the child *assumes* the parent feels about him. In other words, a parent seldom shows deliberate acts of violent hostility. The pressure of community and self-disapproval would force most such strong negative feelings out of awareness. Whether a parent knows these feelings within himself or not, we can be sure the child will know and recognize them. The child may respond with the same negative impulses; yet he will find it necessary to block these impulses. The community will not approve an expression of strong father or brother hate. The hidden anger is often a problem for all concerned.

The son's response to the feeling that his father is hostile or that he gives the blessing to another son can be quite varied. The following are some possibilities. He can turn to his mother for her protection and consolation. Again he can turn to her for assistance in retaliation. He can deny that he feels hostility and act as if things were all in good order. He can turn to a grandparent or grandparents (if they have not indeed already turned to him), or to another brother or sister. He can punish by becoming friendly with the neighbor whom the father distrusts. He can develop hobbies that are completely different from his father's. He can move toward a vocation that

32

his father dislikes. He can do much to express anger in the choice of friends, in the way he wears his clothes and cuts his hair, or doesn't cut it!

This common lot of hostility held between father and son is quite natural. They frustrate each other. The father dreams of what he will do with and for his son; the son responds as if the father were doing things *to* him. On the other hand, the son attempts to plan his life and choose his friends. He might run into two or three generations of plans for his future. These plans could include everything from vocation to matrimony.

The parent usually sees his part in the relationship as a purely wholesome interest in helping the child. The child feels it as great enmity, since it tends to thwart his full expression of selfhood. Hence what the parent feels is blessing, the child feels as rejection.

A case will serve to illustrate the power of this parent-child feeling as it introduces problems for later years.

THE CATS IN THE CANE FIELD

A woman approaching the middle years came to discover that she lived in dread of childhood terrors. While she knew she could manage life with some competence, she still had this lingering or haunting material stalking her path from the early years. There were long periods when it would go away; at other times it would return like a furtive cougar.

In her earliest memories of childhood she felt deeply at one with her father. Her mother seemed unhappy with her own relationship to her husband and children. She said, "Mother was more of an outsider." The mother had forced the stepson by a previous marriage to leave the home and return to his grandparents. She would not keep him. Apparently the father was warm toward all his children; he tended to give them grace, leaving his wife no choice but to represent firmness to the children. They took this firmness as harshness and felt it somewhat as rejection. She would do to them the same that she had done to her stepson— she would banish them, or put the curse on them. She had the ability to "act like a witch."

Then it happened that the tables were turned. The father took this little girl's kittens and killed them out in the cane field. At this point the mother stoutly protested the father's actions. In some sense this left the child deeply uncertain about whom she could trust. As a small child of three she built her defenses against trusting her mother. Now this turn of events forced her to build defenses against her father's destructive power when she was six. The experience of the cats made her feel that this was what the father was capable of doing to his own family—he could destroy them. The mother had earlier aroused the same doubts in her rejection of the stepson. The child felt she would always need to be on guard against destruction coming from one side or the other. She could not trust herself to tell the difference between love and hate coming from others. What seemed to be hate in her mother finally revealed itself as a protectiveness. What was love in the father finally turned into the power to destroy.

The first childhood resolve (or vow) took the form of sheltering her father from the harshness of her mother. He got so little love, she would see that he got plenty. A few years later a resolve came from the opposite side: she must join with her mother to ward off the "brutal old man." She wanted to give her mother the love she needed.

This woman missed tenderness coming from her mother during her childhood. She gave her father her love and lost her kittens. She came out of the tangle with the determination to be the best mother she could be. The battle of her parents had been that each struggled to lean on the other, yet neither could support the other. The child was determined to make her way by letting others lean on her. As a result she became a compulsive mothering type, inheriting community tasks by the score. She became the all-sufficient mother. But she finally sought help because she could not mother enough or work enough to quiet her fears that were represented by what happened to the half brother and the cats in the cane field. She needed acceptance in her deeper childhood self so she could be freed from a compulsion to mother all the world.

When she began discussing her needs, she became hostile that her parents had continued to depend on her so heavily. She had to go through quite a period of anger about this. Later she began to be herself enough to let them also be what they were. They were both past seventy and were not likely to change. She learned to accept that they either would not or could not change.

She then had to come to terms with her anger toward a God who would not intervene to stop such a complicated emotional tangle. She had always believed that God would "make things come out right."

Her inner and hidden anger toward God was much like the subtle curse she held for her parents. Deeply and fearfully she felt she had to be on guard against all authority in heaven and on earth. Much of the past feeling of curse was lifted as she realized she could have her honest feelings, positive and negative, toward her parents and toward God. She had assumed from childhood that such thoughts and feelings must always be kept out of sight and out of mind. As long as they remained so, they gave her the drive to work in the church and community to get the praise of many people. Voices of praise were like incantations against childhood voices of curse and disapproval. But she had to keep working for it. As she came more to accept the blessing as a gift, she could surrender some of her drive to be pleasing to others.

Pastors who themselves do not feel that the blessing can be bought with work can help break up the slavish hold of the past on a person. They can support others enough for them to take a look at themselves. A person seldom has the ability or the courage to see himself by himself. It sounds unreasonable that a man would be afraid of his child of the past, but he usually is. He needs another person to walk with him into the inner tunnels of fear and mystery, one who is already acquainted with the journey.

TOWARD RELEASE FROM THE VOWS

There is no easy formula for releasing a person from the terrors and fears of early childhood. There are few people who escape at least a partial curse from the experience of being a child. Not many adults can act like adults all the time.

Most adults are not able to "put away childish things."

The pastor is given a rather unusual opportunity to be helpful when a person lives under a feeling of rejection or curse. The pastor is cast in a caring role; he is pictured as a shepherd looking after sheep. This makes trust come a little easier. It can make possible an openness not extended to the ordinary man. This strengthens the pastor's hand to be helpful simply because he is allowed the privilege of closeness.

There are times when the buried material of the early feelings of curse will not yield to a positive pastoral relationship. These are sometimes situations that call for psychiatry. Psychiatry often enters the scene to help a person understand his dragons of the past. But understanding is not enough to bring motivation. One can understand and still live in a stalemate. Pastoral reassurance and care might be the necessary follow-up to charge all the unacceptable past data with a feeling of forgiveness and acceptance. For example, a man coming to see his early murder impulses might have deep guilt that will need a deeper word of affection.

A woman of fifty spent three years working through her early life with a psychiatrist. He helped her understand some strong murder feelings she entertained as a child toward her mother.

The psychiatrist tried to reassure her that this was rather normal and natural. However, she sought out her minister. He brought her the sure and firm word of God's loving acceptance if she could accept it without obligation. She was greatly unburdened and dealt with more such feelings not only from the past, but in the present. The pastor asked why she had not heard the psychiatrist when he gave her some assurance. She replied she knew the psychiatrist to be a religious man, but added, "He has never *studied* God's word and the ways of prayer, and I know that you have." In plain language, it remains true that we are able to do for people what they will allow. The role of pastor was extremely powerful because this woman put so much trust in his discipline in the word and in prayer. The pastor could help remove the curse of the hostile feelings because he could speak the "good news" of acceptance that went to the depths of the child inside the woman.

CHILDHOOD AND THE CURSE OF DEATH

Adults can understand the fact of death and can usually come to terms with it. But preschool children have much difficulty with the subject. Death could be the most unwelcome word in the child's vocabulary. The power to curse and the

39

power to kill are about the same in the world of magic. Every child lives for a time in that world. Primitive man never gets out of it. Rational man gets his mind out of it, but only partially gets his emotions out. A case will illustrate some of the things we are saying.

A man of forty-five sought help from his minister who in turn referred him to a more thoroughly trained pastoral counselor. The man wanted to talk with someone about his past. He explained that he had worked through some of his needs with a psychiatrist for a year and a half. There was one thing he had not brought out that he felt needed the help of religion. When he was sick with flu at six years of age his father went to get medicine for him. On the way home the father was killed in an automobile accident. To make matters worse, only three days before the accident, his father had lost his temper with the son and beat him severely. After the punishment no words had been spoken between them. After telling his story the man said he could never overcome the dreadful feeling he was carrying that he had caused his father's death. He explained the feeling as a tightness in his chest. He also remembered his mother reminding him that the father was on an errand for him when he had the accident. It seemed to him as though the mother never forgot and never forgave him fully. He said his present relation to her was very strained, as it had always been.

To put this in a religious frame of reference, here was a man who needed to confess. He had not actually killed his father, but he carried as much guilt as if he had done so. As soon as he got this guilt feeling out in the open, the pastoral counselor was able to detect his inner cry for a blessing. After the pastor brought blessing to him, the man returned the next time to say that most of the tightness had gone out of his chest.

The loving acceptance of the counselor allowed the man to cry for the first time over the death of his father. He remembered how his hate would not let him turn loose when he attended the funeral of his father. The counselor's acceptance had some power to make up for the long absence of his father's blessing. Following this he was able to get much of the strain out of his relationship to his mother after some thirty-three years.

This all says that man is one piece, past and present. He is indeed a "part of all he has met." His child of the past is always at work to avoid hurt, to find new meaning, new relations, and new powers that will bring peace, self-acceptance, and fulfillment. Where a man must be in retreat from past fears, he is not likely to be open to reality and truth. He is denied the kind of growth that is needed if he holds most of his emotions under some strong shield of protection. Meaningful religion can help bring freedom from earlier powers of curse if it can assure a person of acceptance and mature love.

II

Curse and Blessing in Childhood

The child is no stranger to violent emotions. They are not easy for him to manage; in fact, they leave him with inner turbulence that may take many years to resolve, if indeed it is ever resolved. Children have to go through the stormy climate of the home and the community. Parents, older children, relatives, and neighbors feel the pressures of the outside world, and these pressures reach to the very covers of the cradle. These things include the frictions in the home and the many annoyances and anxieties that flow back and forth from the spheres of politics, economics, and social life. They include cold and hot wars, nuclear threat, racial strife, educational turbulence, labor troubles, inflation, air and water pollution, high interest rates, traffic congestion, crowded living, poverty, public health and safety, organized crime, and delinquency.

The infant is in some sense exposed to all these pressures and many more long before they can be realities for him. The people who love and care for him are moved by and often controlled by some or all of these unseen, outside, and often hostile currents. These powers strongly influence parents as they take up the sacred responsibility of raising a child. They work their way into the very hands that lift and cuddle him. The society around the child has already been at work trying to make life more stable for him against the ebb and flow of the devouring and dangerous forces.

At best the infant is born into a situation of stress and conflict. Men have not learned how to master the evils of nature and society, and they cannot completely protect their children from them. Indeed no child would be ready for living responsibly if he was thoroughly protected from all these outer realities. On the other hand, a child has fewer chances to cope with life if he is overexposed in tender years.

A child can get caught up in the conflicts that put a feeling of curse upon him as he strives to relate to realities and as these realities invade his sphere of life. These conflicts include the curse of (1) being dependent, (2) of being independent, or measuring up to the demands of others, and (3) of coming to terms with the big questions of where he came from and where he is going.

THE CURSE OF DEPENDENCY

The right of self-determination is the cry of persons as well as nations. "I want to do it myself" is the child saying he wants to "do his own thing." Yet the child awakens to his world as one that has designs on him. It wants to take him into a life that is already planned and programmed for him. In fact, there are many competing voices that plead, seduce, or promise.

From the earliest awareness that these expectant feelings are placing a kind of claim upon him, the child begins to declare his independence. He may enjoy the attention and feeling of importance he gets out of this, but he begins to protect himself against the *total* claim of any other person or power.

He wants love without being devoured, and freedom without being abandoned.

The child is in conflict within himself in that he hungers for the kind of love he got as an infant, while, at the same time he sets some boundaries around his personhood, thus creating a barrier

45

to love. This starts the process that will help him venture from the mass that is his home and his security to the space that is his uncertainty and his freedom.

The pressures from without (parents, school, church) join with those within himself to nudge the child away from ever being completely helpless as he once was as an infant. This could be one of his earliest vows—the vow to be strong and independent, to be self-sufficient never to need another that much again.

The craving of the child for tender love becomes a problem for him as he tries to "be big like brother." He never outgrows his need to depend, yet that need can be felt so strongly that it becomes frightening. The more it is felt, the more it must be denied. This can best be handled by showing more independence; by not letting oneself or others see that it would be so good to roll the calendar back and lose the pressures of competition for a while.

This is illustrated in the behavior of the ulcer patient. On the one hand, he is the executive type who literally takes care of a lot of people. Yet he has a difficult time allowing anyone to take care of him while he is sick. The hospital picture so often is that of a strong and vigorous looking man lying fitfully upon his bed while being subjected to a kind of mothering process. The formula

46

is in a bottle or pack near his bed and a woman in white comes regularly to see that he gets his food in the right amounts. While all this is going on he is arguing with the doctor to dismiss him and let him get back to the office. One seems to hear another message just below the spoken one. It would go something like this: "Doctor, you have to get me out of here. This is just too good to be true. If I stay here I will become wed to this room so that I can never turn it loose. Quick, help me by not letting me see that I need to be cared for. I have too many others leaning on me to think about my needs. Besides all this, I'm no baby, and I'm too important to others to spend my time like this. Discharge me before I get addicted to the care. I love it so much, I can handle it only if I remain a teetotaler."

No one can come through the first year of life without many frustrations. These include many real needs that may be momentarily blocked because the mother cannot meet them as fast as they build up. For example the child could cry for sleep, for food, for a show of love, and for relief from diaper burn all at the same time. He usually expresses his needs in a protest of anger. The caring mother moves with dispatch to provide for his needs as best she can. The minor frustrations are not serious. But if there are the major

47

frustrations of little love, poor nutrition, and frequent anxiety in the home, the child will develop a deep protest against an unfriendly environment. He will come out of the first year ill prepared to move into the next phases of development. He will likely have much unspent rage that will follow him—he will have the core material of curse.

The child who moves fulfilled out of the first year will not have as much need to return to it. Without fulfillment, there remains a need to go back in order to recover what he missed. His homesickness is for a time that cannot return and for a place that has vanished.

The adult who is very dependent could be wearing emotional braces against some injury and frustration from the beginning months of life. It is seen plainly in some patients who take the posture of the unborn baby as they lie about the wards of a mental hospital. Again it is a problem with those who lean heavily on other people for this emotional support. A minister often faces this problem with a number of people. He will experience it with the alcoholic or the drug addict. It is not uncommon for these people to surrender the drug or the alcohol and replace them with the supportive affection of a pastor. It is better to be addicted to people—we all are, but cannot afford to let it show too much.

The man with a strong need to be dependent

will reveal it in literally scores of ways. It shows up in his marriage as a need to blame his wife for all the ills of life. (This may be his deepest kinship to Adam!) He may little recognize that while he accuses and blames he still leans on her for much support. Often this will include financial support. He will sometimes be incapable of accepting the first child, especially if this is a son. He may take the position of rival and show intense jealousy of his wife's attention to the child. I hasten to add that all the sons of Adam react this way to some extent!

Dependency shows up in fear or lack of drive in the adult. Again it is revealed in a need to sleep long hours or to eat excessively. Others express it in a kind of voraciousness in their relationships; they tend to devour the people to whom they relate. The dependent person wants people around him. He uses the telephone to excess and uses it to wrap himself around others to the point of annoyance. His talk is often excessive and without significant content.

The need for approval is another quality often seen in the very dependent person. It will take the form of his being ingratiating to the point of manipulation. He will not risk losing love by showing his true feelings. He speaks the flattering word. He compliments the minister on his sermon in flowery terms and will not be able actually to discuss its contents. In the fear of his "nay" he speaks "yea." He tries to bless with flattery, and that is only a half-blessing while the curse (or should we say the half-curse?) is held inside.

There is no essential curse in being dependent. The problem comes in our not being able to accept that the child is still within the man. That inner child will cry out for his own hungers if he is stifled. But this expression will be hidden as was the case with the ulcer patient. He gets his tender love with such protest he cannot really let himself enjoy it. He cannot even accept what is happening. The curse comes in declaring war on the voices and vows of childhood, as if they had to be driven into limbo in order to let this particular man keep up his image of being the one who has no need to lean on others.

The gospel recognizes the need of man to come to terms with the childhood past in saying that one enters life in becoming like a little child. Isaiah pictures the caring God over Israel as ministering to the very infant in the soul of every man:

> And you shall suck, you shall be
> carried upon her hip,
> and dandled upon her knees.
> As one whom his mother comforts,
> so I will comfort you.
>
> (Isaiah 66:12-13)

THE CURSE OF INDEPENDENCE

The curse of independence is only the flip side of the coin of the curse of dependency. The addiction in independence tends to fix on law, rule, conduct, good behavior, and the like: "Cursed be everyone who does not abide by all the things written in the book of the law, and do them" (Galatians 3:10). It becomes the "curse of the law." That curse comes in living under the assumption that one can work the magic charm in life by his own high, good, or holy conduct. The danger in dependency is that of being devoured in getting love; the danger in independence comes in putting rules ahead of people or the Sabbath ahead of man.

"Bless me and let me go" is the image of being freed in a good sense. The blessing is a kind of sending forth; it is the word that cuts the dependent and binding ties to one's home or one's country. It is the word of the father that releases his son. It is the Father of the Prodigal Son giving the son his share of the goods. It is the power in which Abraham went out. Jesus sent his apostles in the power of his blessing (the Great Commission). The church at Antioch took Barnabas and Paul: "Then after fasting and praying they laid their hands on them and *sent them off*" (Acts

51

13:3). They went with the blessing, and in the strength of it.

It is very important to many young couples that they get the "blessing" of parents (and church) in marriage. Where there is no blessing the venturing out is often an attempt to find blessing somewhere else. This is seen in a professional man whose father disappeared from the home when the children were small. It was reported that the father lived as a vagabond and a tramp. This particular man could not restrain himself from going to bars where he would invariably get into conversation with some needy transient and elderly man (looking for the blessing even there?). He said on one occasion that he would give all he had if he could find his father.

Many people do go without blessing, and of course most of them find ways of coping with life. They chiefly make their claim upon life in the name of what they *do*. Yet there is frequently a secret underground or hidden hold of the past that tends to enslave the person who must force himself into proving his own worth by his works and good efforts. The unblessed independence may be only a sham; at least it lives in the illusion that it will finally earn enough or achieve enough to return and claim the blessing fully. It takes a freeing love to help a man to go or even to help a child grow—in the better sense.

52

Independence is a healthy and worthy goal for any child to assume. If he accepts it he does not have to give up all his dependency. But if he takes it as an absolute demand, he is unable to wear it loosely and comfortably.

Sometimes parents attempt to push a child toward functioning that is ahead of his ability. They expect him to be months head of the cousin or neighbor the same age. Where this happens they tend to demand that he be perfect in all his ways. They want a *good* child, hence they draw strong limits of the *bad* in warnings and all manner of disapproval (personal and physical).

This is the child's encounter with law, control, and limits. Whereas in infancy he was loved as he existed (by grace), he comes now to feel that he is loved if he conforms (by law). Since he must shape up to get his love, the child must give up being a child. *He begins then to be the blessing for his parents* (and this is a curse!). He is expected to perform, to act, to achieve, to stage himself, to be cute, or to recite. He must strive to meet adult demands to the point that he cannot be himself.

The parent who imposes the law in the form of his own past vows on his child is not accepting the child. As long as these vows dominate, true growth toward mature independence is all but impossible. A couple of examples of this will point up the problem better. One man said he would give his children the things he never had as a poor farm boy. He worked at two jobs to provide the comforts he never had. His children got none of his time and very little of his love, but much of his law. They wanted and needed the love most of all. He was frustrated that they did not constantly see how "blessed they were" by all he had provided. One by one his three sons dropped out of high school and became juvenile delinquents.

A woman had lost her mother as a fourteen-year-old girl. She was the eldest of four children and had to be a mother to the other children while their father moved into alcoholism. She took a vow to "have a perfect home when I married." She could only tolerate perfection, and she demanded it of her husband and two children. The husband retreated from her into drinking, and her son was killed in an automobile accident while drunk. Her only daughter got pregnant and married at fifteen to get away from this "perfect home." Her legalism was given without much love.

Children are unable to see the vows their parents drag along from the past. If they could see them, it is doubtful that they could accept them. This is seen in a man who failed in medical school. He was determined to have a son become a doctor because his father had always wanted him to be a doctor. Since he had let his father down, it would be done in the next generation. The son got the M.D. degree and handed the diploma to his father. He then returned to college to major in history, which was his own interest. He kept his father's vow in the letter but not in the spirit.

In the above illustrations the vows became curses upon the children. Because of them the children could not be free; the past vows of parents tied the children's feet so they could not move freely along the path of growth, maturity, and independence. No doubt these children were left enslaved to their own vows that were made to take the place of the absent blessing—the blessing that could have sent them out with some inner peace to a mature separation and uncursed independence.

After the child meets with law and limits in the family he then comes to deal with the great mysteries of his beginning and end—where he came from and where he is going.

ORIGIN AND DESTINY

A child's questions about where he came from and what they did with grandpa at the funeral usually make parents anxious. Where there is anxiety the child tends to work out his own answers, and these are seldom gratifying. Where these areas become "off limits" for discussion the child gets the idea that he has discovered the forbidden fruit.

It is interesting that we have traditionally interpreted the forbidden fruit as sex. This is not so much openly taught as *felt*: that because of sex Adam had to die. Again it is not taught that God decided to kill Adam for what he did, but it is *felt*. God then becomes the power of the curse because he will not tolerate sexual feelings. The child somehow comes to think that he can avoid the curse only if he can put away his thoughts and questions as well as all feelings having to do with this forbidden subject. Of course the more he is constrained to do this, the more the thoughts and fantasies creep in.

Sex is essentially a very powerful feeling, but it does not have to be forced into limbo for the child to be accepted and loved. Yet if he feels he must be rid of sexual references in his speech or thoughts in order to avoid the curse and get the blessing of love, he will at least strive to be nonsexual. This of course becomes another point along the journey where he will try to measure up through denial of part of his being. The child will do what he must to get love, but since sex feelings mingle with his love feelings, it is possible for him to go through a kind of spiritual emasculation in order to be spared (loved or saved). It is easy to see that this process can leave a child feeling that he has an inner demon that may at some point erupt from the depths to embarrass or even destroy him. In time he may forget *what* the demon is, but he can hardly for *that* it is.

It is difficult, if not impossible, for a child to get through the preschool years without having to imprison some of his anger, sex curiosity, or fears about death. These all tend to make him feel unacceptable in the dark side of the spirit. This is where love can cover a multitude of sins, and it can cast out fear. It is for the reason of casting out fear that the Good News needs to be spoken through the family in loving acceptance of the child.

A man forty-seven years of age related his strained relationship to his father. The father had died fifteen years before, and as he talked about it he gripped his hands until they were white, saying, "The old man died and never once told me he loved me." He was holding on tightly as if to repeat the words of the ancient Jacob wrestling with the angel and saying, "I will not let thee go except thou bless me." It happened that the man's first son was born the day his father died. He had consoled himself with the thought that perhaps the son was sent to be a blessing in the vacuum of the father. A shattering thought broke in as he was relating this: "What do you know, my son is now fifteen years old and I have never told him I loved him." He was pushing that son to be his blessing, and the son was failing in every way to fulfill the desire.

THE CRY OF ESAU

The cry goes up everywhere, the cry for the blessing. The story is written over and over: "a certain man had two sons," and—one of the sons speaks—"My brother could do no wrong," or "My brother was good at sports, and that's what my father wanted," or again, "My brother got his name and I suppose everything else he wanted," or still another, "He was always there when my brother called, but he didn't even show up for my wedding." The cry is the cry of Esau, "Have you but one blessing, my father? Bless me, even me also, O my father" (Genesis 27:38).

Esau went out with a vow to kill his brother Jacob. The sons of Esau are still hurling the ancient curse across the Jordan in artillery duels. The sons of Ham are weary of the curse—not the curse of God, but the curse of the white man. He is shouting that curse back across the campuses and in the labor halls. Maybe he is trying to say that he is a son, too, and he wants the blessing. Wherever there is cursing, there is a response to a curse. Hitler vowed to remove the curse of the West from the German nation. Is it really strange that

58

he would annihilate the "people of the blessing" —the Jew? The youth of China are given a vow against two big brothers, the Americans and the Russians—the vow is to destroy. This vow will be more serious when these youth come of age and political leadership.

Our children cannot escape the swirling cross-currents of the political, social, and economic world. They will hear the curses in the streets and in the schools. Their vows are being shaped either in terms of returning curse for curse or in accepting the Good News that says the blessing is with those who can endure the curse without cursing back (Matthew 5:11).

III

The Depths of the Curse

The pastor will not use the knowledge he has
gained through intense study of the Word of
God, the nature of prayer, and the hard-earned
results of the psychological study of persons in
the same way the doctor will use his knowledge.
Each will benefit to the degree that it helps him
understand himself. In his professional applica-
tion of such knowledge, the doctor will sometimes
move deeply into the feeling life of his patient.
His knowledge of psychology will assist the doctor
in helping a patient lower his guard enough to
see and understand himself better. The minister
will use a deeper understanding of others to give

him more patience and skill in relating to them. He will know better how to get off his own guard. He will know how to listen to troubled people with less risk of rejecting them in their weaker moments. The person who goes to the pastor for help will often fear that the pastor will tell him to do what he cannot do. The same man going to a doctor might fear the doctor will allow more freedom than he can manage.

The pastor with good insights into the lives of people will be more able to affirm them in his affection in spite of their unloveliness or their failures. He will be more able to help them change, and at the same time he will be more able to accept them when they are unable to change much.

As an understanding shepherd, the pastor will be a reflection of the gospel's image of God. He will come to his people with an open hand rather than with a pointed finger. He will learn how to give himself in a more skillful way so as to bring help to the anxious or the guilty person. In so giving he will find his own replenishment and renewal.

A cry has gone up from ministers in modern society that they are constantly under too much pressure to do too many things. The wise minister will know how to weed out the trivia. He will give more of his time where he can see meaningful results. He will be able to leave the ninety and nine who make unhappy noises and spend useful time with the one who is quietly withering under the curse, famished for the blessing.

We continue, then, toward taking a look at some of the people who are harassed and helpless while they long for the light of hope or even a ray. These factors are of more value than administrative or financial consideration. They should be heeded above attendance records and the stewardship problems, which in themselves may be cold testimonies to people's alienation and their fear that they may not be able to enter into life and fulfillment.

ANXIETY

Anxiety is a problem of the human spirit. It so overloads one's spirit at times that the glands and tissues of the body become the dumping ground (the gehenna) of its poisons. Anxiety enters when intense pleasure is offered with intense pain, where blessing and curse surround the same act or circumstance. It is the leap into uncertainty, the hope of great reward and fear of loss. It is living where "the stakes are high." It is leaving our mass of security for a space unexplored. It is Abraham going out not knowing.

The tension of anxiety builds up over most things in life. One may be led to feel that money is one of those things that brings pure pleasure. Yet most people are anxious over money—it offers pleasure *and* pain. It promises to serve but it soon becomes master; thus it makes us anxious. It promises respite from privation, but possession of it brings neighbor or brother to scorn. Hence, one becomes anxious to obtain the right amount, though nobody can tell what that amount is.

The same thing can be said of the management of sex. As a feeling it promises blessing; as an idea it threatens as if to curse. There is both the promise of fulfillment and the danger of rejection all wrapped up in the handling of this drive.

In the very beginning weeks of life a child can develop anxiety in relation to his mother. She may easily represent this same pattern—his greatest pleasure and his sharpest disappointments, frustrations, or pains. She represents both bottle and paddle. In some sense she will be the symbol of his anxiety. She may not even know whether he is crying to get her help or to avoid her presence if she is anxious.

Anxiety is the facing of decision, to be or not to be. It is a clutching of all the securities available although knowing that ultimate security comes in turning loose. Anxiety is the "leap of faith." It is leaving father and mother. Basically it is leaving a mass for a space.

Anxiety may be experienced as a chronic souring

of the spirit. Again it will show up as a sweaty palm, dilated pupils, crawling of the skin, tightness in the throat, or butterflies in the stomach. It is usually felt as stress upon some organ or function of the body. These will include frequent urination, diarrhea, peristalsis of the bowel, or even blurred eyesight.

Anxiety may be felt as fear, but it is more than fear. Fear is related to an object of threat that can usually be identified. Anxiety tends to have no object, or it has a poorly defined object. It tends to be the fear of fear itself, running when no one pursues. It may be characterized in the astronaut who delights in the glory of a space venture while he worries about lift-off, weightlessness, separation from mother earth, and all the mechanical problems of the capsule, together with the terrifying stress of re-entry. All the while, all systems are clear while thousands of others work day and night for his safety. Yet he is anxious. If he let it rule him, he would only write space fiction as to how it *might* have been without the curse of fear.

Anxiety tries to keep open all the doors of possibility without closing any of them. It shuns decisive action. It puts off becoming one thing because it wants to be all things. In this sense it wants to be like God—assuming he is able to be all things. Hence it sweats, it complains, it aches,

64

it writhes, and it spreads itself into any or all systems of the body, creating symptoms in abundance. Anxiety has its causes. It develops as a person grows. The forerunner of most anxiety is guilt. Behind the guilt there is anger. Going further back, behind anger there is frustration. The following case will serve to show the progression from one of these factors to the next.

Inez G., a college student in her junior year, sought help from a minister because she had trouble relating comfortably to other people. She said she saw herself making awkward and inappropriate responses and was unable to control these actions. The result was that she could not keep a boy friend and could not get along with her roommates. She drove people away without meaning to do so. She had the feeling there was something terribly wrong with her and she did not know what it was. She lived in constant anxiety with a number of symptoms. These included bursitis, frequent headaches, diarrhea, and dizziness. There was also a problem of acne.

As she told the story of her life, she related that she was the elder of two children. There was a brother three years younger. When she was six years of age her parents took a niece from a broken marriage. The niece was two months older than Inez and was a much more comely child. As Inez talked about this cousin she thought her parents

65

had done a noble thing. She defended them more than the occasion demanded. When she started to discuss her father she began to weep. She did not know why there would be so much guilt in talking about him. He had been the more noble in taking the niece since it was actually his wife's niece. He had gone the extra mile to treat the niece as his own child. The more she talked the more she felt guilty.

It is easy to see the frustration behind the anger here. Inez was frustrated in her affection, and she was denied the right to her parents as her very own. In addition she felt the pain of competition with the cousin for playmates. She usually came off second. Then the money for clothing had to be divided, leaving Inez with fewer dresses than she needed.

In her frustration Inez was not able to know her own feelings. Her true feelings as a child had to be concealed or repressed. Her parents set things up for the cousin with no explanation and no discussion with Inez. Inez even came to college with the feeling that her parents were right. They were always right. She could not bear to think her own independent thoughts about them or her cousin. This meant she repressed her frustration and her hostile feelings before they could even come near the surface of recognition. This began when the cousin came into the home, and it did not change until Inez began to get to the deeper material in counseling. Her anxiety had produced enough trouble in her relationships to push her for help. She was able finally to accept that she was not "bad" because of her frozen anger. When she could thaw it out she moved out of her fear to give and receive affection. She realized God could love and bless her; in this assurance she began the process of trusting others and relating without such caution.

GUILT

Guilt can flow into anxiety and escape recognition of itself. It can express itself under the label of anxiety. The same is true of hostility and frustration. Most of the powerful emotions can be held in until they are not recognized in their own name. They can ride piggyback on other emotions. Guilt is a particularly unpleasant feeling. Very few people are able to say simply, "I am guilty." It is much less incriminating to admit anxiety.

When guilt is driven into exile, it usually returns to power in the vestments of anxiety. Anxiety attempts to socialize or exteriorize guilt in some disguised form. For example, Lady Macbeth showed her excessive anxiety in her hand-washing compulsion. But the guilt of the blood of King Duncan was on her hands. Hence her guilt was exposed in the symptom her anxiety selected. The waters of anxiety are not usually deep enough to cover the traces of guilt.

Guilt is the recognition of failure to keep the accepted code of the moral law. This recognition of failure can come in disapproval from others or from the self. It is the awareness that the self is under judgment of the self and others.

There is another source of guilt that comes from nothing other than growing up. There is much guilt in surpassing the father in physical stature, in education, in sophistication, and in financial position. There is a kind of primitive assumption that the son is not to surpass the father. When he does so in any way he usually feels guilty. This is not to say the son should be limited by his father, or that the son should restrain his impulses to venture and grow. The fact that the son will feel guilt in passing the father in any or all dimensions should be no deterrent to his strivings. Primitive cultures handled this conflict by exalting the father, the grandfather, and the patriarchs of the past. Christianity set the stage for family and social revolution by mustering the courage to make the son equal to the father—"Call no man your father."

In order to understand this problem of guilt over growing, we must begin with the fact that the child, between three and six years of age, tends to absolutize his parents. They are the gods on Olympus. As the child grows the gods start the inevitable process of decline. The child simply cannot prevent this crashing of his idols as he moves toward adulthood. The nursery rhyme of Humpty-Dumpty expresses the crumbling of the parental clay feet—once they have been seen, there is no going back. This is the truth of Thomas Wolfe's *You Can't Go Home Again*. It is also the midnight hour in the story of Cinderella. This is the signal of reality that brings the fantastic to a halt; it turns the carriages back to pumpkins and the horses to mice. The child can no longer live completely in the world of fiction after he loses the fairies and Santa Claus. He knows he is in the process of reaching to take his father's place. This cannot be done apart from guilt feelings. Note that in the case of Inez, there was guilt over bringing into question the parent's actions in making the niece equal to Inez, the daughter. Even the thought of their being anything short of perfect was threatening to her. It became necessary for her to repress her own deep feelings and thoughts, and hence to live with her own self-imposed curse.

REPRESSION

Repression is in many respects a respectable term for the curse. A person will voice it as "the thing that keeps me from having forgiveness," "some quirk in my makeup," "the shadow over our family," "the awful feelings I keep having," or "something I can't understand that keeps bugging me." It is the demon of the New Testament, the witchcraft of the Middle Ages, and the persistent fear in many of being illegitimate or the spiritual kin of trolls, gnomes, sprites, and goblins. So often these things do not bother the sophisticated and cultured man of modern times until the sleepless hours after midnight, or a serious accident, or his awaiting the results of a biopsy. Then we see the wife of an esteemed physician consulting a palmist, or a renowned clergyman swapping his vestments for the swirling sheets of the soothsayer.

Modern dynamic psychology has labored to understand these primitive fears, and it has helped to enlighten our knowledge of the curse. It holds that painful, threatening, and humiliating experiences can be buried below the conscious memory. This is more true of a child than of an adult. Hence, repressions that give most trouble in an adult are those of the childhood years. They are the many and varied experiences that a child is unable to manage through simple understanding and growth. Among the more troubling ones are sex and death. Perhaps the chief reason these are unmanageable is the amount of anxiety they stir in the parents. If parents cannot interpret them, the child cannot deal with them!

The child starts with the assumption that his parents can read mind and thoughts. If he has a series of unacceptable thoughts, he must hide his eyes from the unapproachable light in the father's eye. The father's is the all-seeing eye. He could be the "beast with a thousand eyes" to the guilty and self-conscious child. The more typical handling of the problem is to get the guilt out of the eyes by forcing the material completely out of mind. This allows the child to come into the father's presence without wrinkled brow and squinting eye. He banishes from memory the offenses that he assumed would bring punishment or even annihilation. With the child the guilt is about the same in an imagined offense as in a real one. The big, powerful adult is one who can read the "thoughts and intents of the heart."

Let me repeat: Repression is largely a process of putting out of sight and out of mind the unacceptable childhood feelings. They include fury, hate, or even murderous rage. But the child cannot bury the crime (or curse) without continuing to feel some threat of exposure.

Fear and anxiety are the repressing energies. They encase the unacceptable thoughts. For a person to get back to the hidden material, he must penetrate these layers of fear and anxiety.

71

Indeed he will relive the same degree of fear he had when he repressed the experience, even if it comes out fifty years later. If he felt the material was cast off on pain of death, he will recall it in a like fear of death. We should emphasize that children can make capital cases out of small issues. If the material is approached many years later, the adult will go through terror. The terror is not over the size of the offense that was buried; it is over the amount of fear that was layered around it in the original assumption that the offense would bring curse.

Repressions are the experiences that cannot be made a part of one's life. They are literally the hard lumps one had to swallow. Since they are not made workable through understanding, they are placed in secret chambers and held in place with the energy of fear. These lumps, or repressions, want to come to light and understanding. They form the material of many dreams and nightmares. They are often the cause of phobias, free-floating anxiety, and much of man's feeling that he is "cut off out of the land of the living."

The buried material is never free to return directly to awareness. It often will manifest itself in illness or some symptom. The symptom is an attempt to speak without really revealing anything. It can be the outcropping of a rash, following a pattern of rash behavior. It can be a bloodstained Lady Macbeth compulsively washing her hands until the physician says: "Infected minds to their deaf pillows will discharge their secrets."

Repressions are the power within a man that make him work against all his avowed and willful intentions. They are strong because they are deep in the vows of the child of the past. The adult is simply unable to will them away. The wise minister will not lose his patience when he sees good Christians doing things they actually do not want to do. These include such things in children as taking money, bed-wetting, or nail-biting when they likely deplore all this in themselves. A repression might manifest itself as fear of heights, fear of bridges, fear of cats, fear of water, or any number of things. It also takes form as a compulsion to keep order, a compulsion to wash, to step over the cracks, or to walk on the grass.

Because of repression, man has a host of demons within him. They are not the demons that reside under the chips and rocks and jump out to plague man as was pictured in some primitive cultures. They are his own personal demons that took shape when he began saving himself by denying his frightening thoughts and feelings.

The more frightening the hidden feelings become, the more a person tends to withdraw from others. The more he withdraws, the more he tries to work out his problems alone. The more he needs others, the more he denies that he does. He feels cursed and rejected by them and is unable to imagine that others or God could love and bless him unless he could cast out his own demons. This puts a person in a position of trying to save himself by making himself more worthy to receive love. If he could do it by himself, he would really be in worse trouble because he could establish the fact to himself that he did not need others or God after all. He needs blessing to realize that the core of his selfhood is not under curse and banishment because he is hounded by these hidden fears. Until love and blessing come, a person tends to call his very self by the name of the worst that is within him. When these come, they perform a surgery that helps separate the self and the curse.

The curse is also related to the problems of frustration and anger. We will consider some of these.

FRUSTRATION AND ANGER

In the case of Inez G. there was very little awareness that frustration and anger were even in the picture of her relationship to her parents. Since none had even been felt or experienced, it seemed strange to her that these feelings could come out some fifteen years later.

74

It may seem rather unreasonable to point to anger if there is no recollection of it. Yet if there was frustration for any reason, there was anger. Anger follows frustration with regularity. Any child faces continuous frustration with his parents. Although it is true that they do the most toward meeting his needs, it remains impossible for them to meet all his needs and wishes. When they fail in this, the child feels frustration. He may or may not be able to allow his frustration to flow into anger. The natural thing in infancy is anger and protest against the least frustration.

By the third or fourth year of life, the child is often prevented from the open protest he was able to express earlier. This comes about as the child becomes aware of parental anger and threat. The child may come to feel that the parent will go so far as to exercise the full powers of life and death over him; this is the last word in power to curse. The child will often think the forces to kill and to curse are so strong he cannot let his emotions spill over as he did in infancy. This is the point where he begins to curb his show of frustration and anger. It seems to him that he cannot continue to survive along this path.

To the small child parental authority is often so threatening that it commands respect, compliance, and even love. It can order a sister to take a cousin as her own sister. It can establish

75

a kind of moral order of its own in its little world. It can deny a child the right to get angry. The threat that is most often used on children is the threat of withdrawing love. Again it can take the shape of offering the child more love if he shows more worth. The hidden assumption may be that he is unworthy and unlovable and should do something about it, especially something about his anger. All he can do at a young age is to deny it open expression. He even tells himself it does not exist.

When the pattern of burying anger is fixed in early childhood, it tends to continue through adolescence and into adult life. It shows up in the adult in many ways. The adult tends to be more compulsive where he had a heavy hand of authority over him in the childhood years. This tendency to be compulsive is the response to an inner and unyielding tyrant that has come to replace the absent parent. This means that the authoritarian parent of the past is internalized. He resides as a curbing force and continues to ring the alarm bell of fear at the slightest approach of anger feelings.

The adult who is saddled with this kind of past parental authority may be one who is religious out of an unusual fear of God. To him God may seem more like the threat of a curse. Religion could come to be a work that attempts to stay God's wrath. The greatest work of merit to this particular image of God is that of holding one's anger in check. The inner assumption of this is that God is threatening and wrathful and will not allow man to deal with him as a person.

The man who is afraid of his anger before God will likely be afraid of it in the presence of any and all authority. He is likely to have trouble praying. He is the man who will have difficulty expressing his real feelings to any minister. He will have great difficulty with grief because he cannot allow himself the deeper question of "why."

This man will have so little practice expressing his feelings that he will be afraid of his anger. He may tend to think about it as a kind of cherished and powerful explosive that he and others are afraid to ignite. He agrees with himself that he should withhold this earth-shattering anger so as to protect others from some kind of lethal exposure. His anger is not really all that powerful and would not do much damage in a full discharge. He tends to keep his fantasy about a dangerous anger. He does this by not testing it in a real situation. He prefers to hold it inside and assume that he is virtuous by doing so. All the while he may be deluding himself about the actual tonnage of thrust behind his rage. He will all the more need situations where he can learn the plain but humiliating fact that his anger is not as powerful and dangerous as he thought. He needs to learn that it does have much power to destroy him if it is held inside. Hence the truth is that a man's anger, his "yea" and his "nay," can be expressed without as great a hurt to others as he feared.

If the minister gets a man's "yea" but never his "nay," he will know that anger is kept inside. He may or may not do anything to get at the deeper problems of frustration and repression. But he needs to know a healthy person is not one who is under a compulsion to speak only sweet and agreeable things.

THE CHANNEL OF BLESSING

Perhaps the best use of insight into the nature of personality for the pastor and the helping person is a better knowledge of his own vows, his curse, and his blessing. Certainly each one has great difficulty with the anger, frustration, repression, guilt, anxiety, and sense of doom that come out of these. Unless he comes to recognize many of these forces working within, the minister will tend to pronounce further doom upon persons in the midst of struggle. He may not do it intentionally so much as unwittingly. He will reject them at the *feeling* level. He will never know why a certain person did not come back to church or why he stopped seeing him as a counselor.

Psychological insight is not enough to give a minister what he needs for his task. Personal reception of the blessing is a prerequisite. One minister said he found his renewal when he both discovered and accepted that he had to go the same route for grace that he taught his people. He had assumed they could get theirs through repentance and faith, but unknowingly assumed he would have to strive for approval by first making himself pleasing to God, especially as a "sweet, nice, affable guy."

If a minister takes the good news of the power of blessing seriously he will be more able to enter into the insights of psychology. He will have been laid hold of by a power that is beyond his own manipulation. Insight can make life more miserable unless it is fused with the power of a blessing that neutralizes the demonic forces by a strong capacity to receive as well as give love and blessing.

IV

The Curse of Taking God's Place

Man does not want to be God. Yet he gets into trouble when he says, "God packed his suitcase and left me when my wife went to the hospital." What or who will take the place of the absent God? Again, when God dies, how does man fill that kind of loss? When God seems to deny man what he wants most, what does man do? When man has done all he knows to remove his feeling of curse, what is his next step? If man has done something he feels God will not forgive, what course can he follow? When God allows the things that bring intense suffering, has he failed man?

Out of these and other questions like them,

man finds himself in the temptation to go ahead and find his own way in spite of all. When God does not make himself known, man often fills in as best he can.

THE TEMPTATION OF EVERY MAN

The Scripture probably never meant to picture Adam's temptation as being different from that of every man. Adam is every man. His temptation had to do with eating the forbidden fruit, but in eating it he was to "be as God" (Genesis 3:5). Traditionally we have said man was under a curse because of Adam's sin. We can accept this only as we see every man in the Garden struggling with his own desire to outlive himself. Each person does this in his own way and in his own peculiar confrontation of an outer world of limits that imposes itself upon the inner world of wish and dream. In this intrusion of outer reality, the child often suffers a kind of spiritual vertigo. He insists that his delusions about reality are not false, and he seeks to hold them intact against truth that would destroy them.

Whether he likes it or not, man finds himself an enemy of the truth about himself and his world. Witness the resistance to Galileo's experiment that proved Aristotle wrong. Aristotle had said that a ten-pound weight would fall ten times faster than a one-pound weight. Galileo had the audacity to climb to the top of the tower of Pisa and test the theory by dropping two such weights together. They fell at the same speed. Galileo was driven from the university for daring to challenge so great an authority as the ancient Aristotle. He was also persecuted for supporting the theories of Copernicus that the earth was not the center of the universe. In like manner Charles Darwin challenged man's absolute separation from the other forms of life on the planet. This brought a great storm of protest. Shortly after Darwin, Sigmund Freud struck from the psychological depths. He propounded a theory of the unconscious life, which he affirmed not only to be very powerful but at the same time beyond man's ability to govern through reason.

These and other discoveries have the effect of drawing greater limits around man's fiction of himself as being the center of things. He resists them by nature just as a child tends to defy his first discovery of limitations or the first imposition of limitations. "Do not touch it lest you die" usually becomes an invitation to experiment.

Any man will deny that he wants to be as God. He will say it is a very ridiculous notion. He will deny that he has ever in the slightest degree entertained the idea of such a thing. If this be true— that man does not fall into temptation trying to be as God—then Adam is different. His sin is different, his problems are different. Hence the story in the Scripture would have nothing to do with man today.

We do not ask the direct and embarrassing question of any man whether he wants to be as God. It is obvious that he does not consciously seek such a preposterous goal. But man should answer this by what he *does*, not by what he *thinks*. What does he say by his life and actions? By his solutions to the sin and death question? In his quest for longevity? Do these, in some indirect way, suggest that man attempts to be more than he is, or other than he is? Do they say how difficult it is for man to be naked before God? Does the feverish activity of life become a new and embossed set of fig leaves? And maybe a defense before the One who sees and knows all? Do these actions manifest attempts to get around the mortality problem? Do they reveal constant attempts at escape from cold, stark reality?

We are assuming that man's spirit imprints itself upon his doings. It becomes a translation problem to hear what his spirit says. It often speaks quite a different language from the conscious, rational self. For instance, the men of Babel said much by the tower they undertook to build. Their efforts revealed the wish that they could establish direct traffic with heaven. Man would no longer have to go through the "valley of the shadow." In one way or another, man still works for the same results in his science, his medicine, and his piety.

So man still searches the tree of life for the hidden (and forbidden) fruit. He is willing for God to have everything except the last word. Man would like to reserve that for himself. Hence he multiplies words without limit, seeking to bring forth *the word:* the truth about himself. A truth that would change the truth—that he is mortal and given to disease, disability, and decay. He tends to take that which is his nature to be his curse. The truth, as revealed, about man is that he seeks to rise above his human limitations. He cannot of himself accept himself. He seeks to get away from what and who he is. He somehow senses the painful contradiction in his being. In the imagination he can take flight into the very heavens. In the flesh he is limited on every side. He is like Plato's picture of a winged horse of eternity teamed with a worn out jade. The flesh is not his curse—that is, his being mortal—yet he takes it to be such and would save himself from it.

The truth about man is that he is a compounding of spirit and flesh, of God and animal. He does not have the choice of being one or the other. He can best find fulfillment in accepting the painful contradiction of his being. This he cannot do alone; he needs a fellowship of other pilgrims who accept their contradiction and his. This is where other persons become a "means of grace," or a bringing of blessing.

THE TEMPTATION RETOLD—SUFFERING

A young pastor was near panic. He called a pastoral counselor to assist him on behalf of a young deacon (twenty-nine) in his church who was seriously contemplating suicide. The counselor knew that this case was too critical and dangerous for him to undertake alone, so he set about arranging for psychiatric help. In the meantime, he agreed to see the deacon in order to interpret the need for his going to a psychiatrist. They sat down to discuss the situation. The following is what they said.

C. Your pastor tells me you want help.

D. Yes, I'm afraid. Twice within the past week I have had the feeling that I could not resist the impulse to kill myself. I've got to have some help. I'm afraid to go through these feelings again. I have a wife and three children and God knows they need me. I've got to keep myself in condition to take care of them.

C. Let me say, Mr. B., that I am not the one to

85

be your chief helper since things are this serious. I have already called Dr. Y. and made an appointment for you as soon as we have talked awhile. You have taken your problem seriously. I want you to know that I am taking it seriously, too. You have acted in the interest of protecting yourself and your family. So in keeping with that wish, I feel you must see a psychiatrist.

D. I know I have to have help. The pastor thought probably you could help me so I wouldn't need a psychiatrist.

C. There's not much choice here, Mr. B. This experience calls for both pastoral and psychiatric assistance.

D. Somehow I feel I need to talk to a minister since I had just been ordained a deacon last month. I just wonder if there's any chance for me?

C. You mean you wonder if you are cut off from God?

D. Yes, I get the feeling there's not anything I can do to put things together right.

D. Mr. B., let me take the time we have to try to explain why I called a psychiatrist. It has to do with putting things together. But let us start where we are. Your pastor trusted me to be of help. You trusted him in coming to me. But are you aware how hard it would be for you to open up and tell me your deepest feelings?

D. I couldn't do that.

C. You couldn't trust me that much right now?

D. I doubt if I ever could.

C. You doubt if you could ever share with anyone your greatest secrets?

D. I doubt it very much. I know I couldn't.

C. Does this mean, then, that nobody really understands you?

D. I don't see how they could.

C. It probably also means that there is some question whether God understands and loves you?

D. Naturally, I wonder if he understands.

C. Now let's look at this another way. You believe in Jesus Christ as the atonement for man's sin?

D. Of course.

C. But, really, wasn't that atonement for the masses? You see, their sins aren't so unique, so different. Yours is so big, so exceptional, it is even doubtful if Jesus Christ could accept it, understand it or forgive it, right?

D. I just don't think anyone could possibly ever understand.

C. But you believe sin must be paid for or suffered for?

D. Certainly.

C. What does it mean, then, that you have a sin God can't handle?

D. Do you suppose I'm doing the suffering?

So Deacon B. went with his pastor to the psychiatrist with a doubt that he could ever share much, but with theologically based reasons for attempting therapy. His pastor stayed with him and literally became his blessing after the man was able to trust his doctor enough to tell him of the things that drove him to such desperation.

It is not easy for Deacon B. or for anyone else to accept the fact that there is a drive within man to pay for sin through his own suffering and possibly his death. This is where one gets in the way of his own salvation. He, in his own suffering, replaces the Christ. He offers a fresh, new, living sacrifice. The original "once for all" sacrifice of Jesus Christ just might not be really trustworthy down in his feelings. There is a chance that God did not comprehend man's deep need today. Man abandons (falls away from) grace whenever he interposes his own sufferings.

Am I saying that suffering has no part in Christian living? Not at all. But I hasten to affirm that salvation is by grace as pure gift of God, not by suffering until we become more mellow or more worthy.

Suffering in and of itself has just as much danger as blessing. There is always the risk that man will construe his pain as part of his payment for grace. Through it he might reckon himself to be deserving of extra favor with God. The danger always lurks in intense suffering that man will put himself alongside of the Christ—on the right hand or the left—or he will put Christ where he wants him for his own convenience.

THE TEMPTATION TO MANIPULATE CHRIST

In Christendom a strange thing has taken place. The churches have elevated Jesus in such a way that he is both exalted and degraded. He is exalted in the fact that he is given the central place of honor, but he is degraded in that he is turned into a kind of mendicant, one who must finally beg for the support of his worshipers.

Then, when a person sheds tears "over" Jesus, he has already put himself above Jesus. On the way to Calvary some women began to weep, pouring out their sorrow at what was happening to Jesus. He forbade this act with sharp rebuke. He would not be wept over. Yet, in Protestant tradition, many people have identified with a Christ who has been upheld to them chiefly as the "Man of sorrows." Aisle walkers in revival meetings are often given the image of a hurting, suffering Christ. Appeals are made for worshipers to respond to Christ's miseries. This is seldom spelled out, but often implied as people are induced to have pity on the Christ and do something for his sake.

In Roman Catholic tradition the Crucifix hardly depicts the image of a risen and reigning Lord. He is more an image of one who is helpless, bleeding, and defeated. All the while he is waiting for the worshiper to feel sorry for him, to have pity on him, to help him. The worshiper is led to think he can help by better living and more generous giving. (I should add that the Crucifix is a reality view of a *man* under the curse of death.)

To be sure, the churches need the approval and support of the people. People are the life of the church—the church is not the life of the people. But if things get turned around here, the church will make itself seem the giver of life and grace. In this way, life and grace are dispensed on the conditions that men make themselves pleasing to a pitiful Christ image. It is not so much taught as implied that if one feels pity for the suffering Christ, then Christ will bless him. Pity for a blessing! Unthinkable!

At this point everything is out of position—

things in heaven and things in earth. No man can endure the pity of another man unless he is a callous beggar. Yet without being aware of it, the church, in its dependence on people for its life, has used and abused the Christ to beg them for their loyalty and support. At the feeling level people could get the notion that they were the chief supporters of the Christ. And some could get the feeling that without their support, care, pity, or whatever, the Christ would fail. When the Good News comes it should not leave a man in doubt about the victory of the Christ—he needs no man's pity or props. His struggle is no longer in doubt. The Christ makes his demands on men for their love and loyalty through the church. The church, speaking in his name, can only judge, command, and accept. It cannot beg, wheedle, or bargain and still remain in the Christ-Spirit.

Again I stress that the church has not consciously sought to control the relationship between men and the Christ. Its intention has been good. Yet its results have been that of "putting" Christ in a mold. This then tends to become group (church) God-management. Wherever God is "put" by men, he is less than God. In other words man does not regulate, barter, or peddle salvation. His words do not add to or take away from the Word. God is the one with the first and last word—Alpha and Omega. Man, through the church, cannot control the God-flow. God may flow through the church, around the church, apart from it, or completely without it. It is his Spirit that is the life of the church and the people.

Mature man in the twentieth century needs to be reassured that the Christ is not a captive of the churches. Certainly the image of a Christ seeking pity commands no respect and no genuine worship.

This view can and must be construed as man's spirit speaking his own need to control the Christ. This puts man "above," therefore superior to, the Christ. Especially is this true when the Christ is viewed weeping for man's loyalty and love. This gives every worshiper a chance (unwittingly) to please (and control) the Christ. Wherever the Christ becomes captive of the church, men have elevated themselves into a position that is more than they can sustain.

The seriousness of the situation is not in what man or the church have done to the Christ. It is, rather, in the thing they have done to themselves. In emasculating the vigorous Galilean—more correctly, in making it look as though this has been done—men and the church are admitting that they have emasculated themselves. Unsexed men *need* pity!

THE TEMPTATION—AS LOSS OF SELF

Somehow the idea has come through that self-denial in Christianity means simply that a man is to give up claim to a vibrant selfhood in order to be a good Christian. The teen-ager hears judgment and even curse upon his sexuality. He trusts that by giving up any right to be an authentic self, he can rid himself of impulses he cannot control. The idea has become widespread that a man's rawest and most earthy impulses must be choked off, denied, or stifled. His earthen vessel is felt to be under such judgment and condemnation that it must be gilded with a gloss of piety.

Then again God is often seen as opposing all man's natural inclinations. Where this is the case, man starts out with the assumption that God disapproves all his honest desires and natural impulses. Hence, one would not be free to pray for what he wanted; he would wait for God to tell him what he must do, the assumption being that God does all initiating directly. In some circumstances it has been thought that a candidate for the ministry was a more likely subject if he had "fought the call"—a draftee seems to be preferred to a volunteer in the Lord's army.

Behind all this is the assumption that God follows a rather rigid blueprint for each man. It becomes the task of man to find out precisely what

THE POWER TO BLESS

God has in mind for him. This conception of God could turn prayer into a struggle with God to get him to show more of the blueprint. This places all the responsibility on man to make contact however he can in order to find out what he is supposed to do. The details are presumed to be with God. In this frame of thinking man's chief end comes in his being so spiritually atuned that he can receive the minutest signals from God about what God intends for him. It is never told how man gets these signals. One man told of how he prayed fervently for God to tell him directly, even verbally, what he wanted. In his wisdom later he said he respected God all the more for not answering in the way he prayed for an answer. He said it would have left him with more problems than ever. First he said he would have had no choice once God spoke. He wondered what would happen if God openly asked him to do what he could not do or did not want to do. (He would have really been under the curse then!) He said also that this would have crippled him for having to go back for further words or proofs in the next crisis of choice. Then he wondered how he would be able to tell others about God talking to him this way. He wondered if God could talk to him without destroying his sanity.

When a person accepts this assumption that his pilgrimage is totally dependent on all the plays being called from the sidelines, there is little opportunity for mature growth and fulfillment. In this case God would have all the responsibility, with man playing at the end of a string.

Man's responsibility in this situation would not be personal, professional, or vocational competence, but spiritual perception. But the question naturally arises about how one comes to spiritual maturity. Is it possessed by the one who neglects skills in order to devote himself only to prayer and devotional meditations? Or does maturity come more to the person who approaches his task of life through commitment of himself to that task (though not neglecting prayer as a part of it all)? Must Galileo retract the great discoveries of truth about God's universe because the men of the church disagree? Are we called on to make that kind of self-denial?

DENYING THE WRONG SELF

We have already indicated that man has difficulty with the deep paradox or contradiction in his being. He is a self on the wing and a self on the ground. He is a child of the heavens and a child of the mother earth. He has little trouble accepting his kinship with angels, but more difficulty accepting that he is also "brother of the brute" (Pascal). There is the self of *fantasy*, and

95

there is the *real* self. The fantasy self is gathered from the personal hopes and dreams of greatness and achievement. It incorporates the ideas of doing great things, of winning the headlines, and showing all the others what a worthy and powerful person one is. The real self, on the other hand, may be a frightened, angry, suspicious, love-starved, and anxious person. One has had no trouble accepting his fantasy self. He resists giving up the pretensions to greatness in order to come down to the shattering reality of accepting his earth-self. But his despair comes in that he takes vows with himself to do so much better later. Hence he puts off the day of reckoning with his limits —his real self. The gap between what he was and what he told himself he would be only keeps getting wider. There has to come a time of denial of one's self in order to affirm the other self.

The apostles who followed Jesus no doubt hoped for an experience through which they would enter the kingdom or in which Jesus would file off the rough edges of poverty and give them a place in the sun. They so identified with Jesus that they forgot to be themselves. No doubt they admired him so much that they took on all his visible actions and mannerisms. Could this have been one of the reasons that Jesus told them it was necessary for him to leave them? Could an apostle become a greater Christian by copying all of Jesus' habits and gestures? Or would the burden still be upon him to be himself? Would Jesus prefer carbons of himself to the real in the apostle?

A child identifies with many others before he can affirm his own being and identity. But the route to reality cannot be along the road of slavishly patterning his life after some other human being. If he does that, his goal would have to be that of finally being just what his idol was. Since one person cannot merge into another, this path can only end in despair. The chief element in that despair would be that one had failed to become himself. Perhaps we can better understand Judas as the apostle who took Jesus so literally as his example that he neglected to be himself. It is interesting to speculate that perhaps Judas was the best carbon Jesus had of himself.

No man comes out of childhood without feelings of curse or fears of having tendencies that would keep him from being respectable. There is usually at least a hidden fear that others could not love or accept one if they knew the whole truth. This is aptly illustrated in the general hospital where patients are facing surgery. They do not fear an operation so much as they fear going to sleep at the hands of others. A frequent question when they wake up centers not on their condition but on whether they have talked much, and what they said. The real question behind it all is, Can I be loved if I am known?

Even if this material is completely hidden from its owner, it is there to push him toward pretending and play-acting. It leads him to measures and methods of avoiding coming to terms with whatever it is. Hence he may go in search of a self that others will accept. Hear the words of Kierkegaard about this:

> For the immediate man does not recognize his self, he recognizes himself only by his dress, he recognizes (and here again appears the infinitely comic trait) he recognizes that he has a self only by the externals. There is no more ludicrous confusion, for a self is just infinitely different from externals. When then the whole of existence has been altered for the immediate man and he has fallen into despair, he goes a step further, he thinks thus, this has become his wish: "What if I were to become another, were to get myself a new self?" [1]

The challenging task for pastors becomes that of cutting off the escape routes from the frightening self. This means that we do not give the reward to the play-actor. Again we are defeated if, in the process, a person takes us for his idol.

[1] Kierkegaard, *The Sickness Unto Death*, trans. Walter Lowrie (Princeton: Princeton University Press, 1944), p. 84.

To be sure, we cannot prevent this happening for a time, but it becomes necessary for the other to see and face for himself the real humanity of the pastor or Christian worker who becomes his idol. Men will finally turn on their idols, and the handling of the process often brings the opportunity of seeing a person come to self-acceptance and personal liberation.

Whenever a man builds his defenses against accepting what and who he is, he is taking God's place. He is forced into the process of creating a new self. To go in search of a different self implies that the Creator did not really give him what he needed most or wanted most. Hence he rejects his gift and sets about to make himself into a more acceptable form. The self-made self tries to improve on the original God-made self. The one who rejects what he is, has become his own god. Like Judas, he will in some way climb to his own private hill over against Calvary and do his own lonely and unblessed suffering.

Section 2

THE POWERS OF
BLESSING AND HEALING

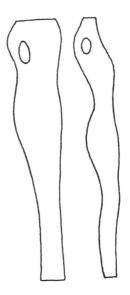

V

The Curse of Grief—and Blessing

"And to Adam he said . . . 'Cursed is the ground because of you; . . . In the sweat of your face you shall eat bread till you return to the ground' " (Genesis 3:17, 19).

Since the day that man saw death as curse he has tried to deal with it as if it might not be a finality and a reality. He has dealt with it as if he just might avoid it by building a tower, by taking a medicine, by transplanting organs, by chemically searching out the secrets of life, or by magically finding a sure way to the unknown in the eerie chambers of the soothsayer. To natural man death is the curse of all curses; it is the father of all fears and the enemy he wants most to conquer.

In spite of all man's efforts to eradicate this great problem, he is repeatedly required to deal with it in one way or another. He is acquainted with his own death in the loss of those he loves and in the loss of the things he loves. Grief is no friendly or welcome guest, but he makes his visits without invitation. Man has the inclination to indulge in unreal solutions to his grief. Yet there are resources by which he can actually turn this great curse into blessing.

THE CHILD AND GRIEF

For the most part, the deepest fears and even horrors surrounding death and grief come in childhood experiences. The man who has grief tends to deal with a present reality of loss, but his feelings of all past grief and losses are often activated. For example, the President of the country is laid low with an assassin's bullet. People gather around their television sets as though they were family altars and weep. They weep for their loss of a leader; they weep for their fathers; they weep for the day they learned that "all flesh is as grass." An event that turns the world's most vigorous leader into a mere piece of clay helps each man realize that he is indeed mortal. His weeping is partly about his own mortality—he weeps for himself.

Present griefs often release unshed tears of the past. Some people are strongly attracted to funerals so that they might discharge old tears under the guise of a new grief. The funeral becomes the umbrella under which are gathered both childhood and adult feelings of pain and loss. Some women in the procession to the crucifixion of Jesus "bewailed and lamented him." Of course their tears were for this occasion, but Jesus freed them to cry for their deeper griefs in saying, "Daughters of Jerusalem, do not weep for me, but weep for yourselves and for your children" (Luke 23:28).

The child, more than the adult, is hurt by grief. It comes when he loses a member of the family, and his solution tends to take the form of a vow. The loss hurts so deeply, he resolves to himself (or his feelings do it for him) that he will not invest himself that much again. He pulls himself back and protects himself. He does not like what grief does to him, so he tries to keep it from being repeated.

Childhood being what it is, the first vow about grief and loss could be forgotten, and the child could put his hurt away enough to gradually open up in renewed trust and warmth. Then it happens again! Needless to say, he will be a lot

longer the next time restoring his trust and returning his feelings.

A woman of thirty-five told of how she lost her
father at six. Her grandfather lived nearby and
came to replace the father. When she was ten,
her grandfather died. She came for help when her
husband was taken to the hospital for emergency
surgery. She told of how she had actually been
afraid to marry because of her fear of his dying.
Now she did not know the cause for all the fears
she was having. She felt the curse hanging over
her, saying: "Everything I love I lose."

A man lost his grandmother and mother in his
early years. He came for help because, he said, he
had such trouble trying to express his love for
his wife. When he got close he was uneasy.

A woman of twenty-five had lost her father
and both brothers while she was a teen-ager. She
was very attractive and had many dates, but said
she just could not get married unless "some man
can give me a guarantee that he will outlive me."

In all these situations there is the curse of grief
hanging on with great tenacity. The adult in each
case is suffering from the "child of the past." The
vow was set: "I'll never love again." The feelings
said, "If you love, you are destroyed."

The child does not even have to go through the
fact of personal loss of a loved one to have terrors
about death that may last many years. All he

106

needs to do is have an exposure to others who wail, mourn, or cry convulsively. This tends to give a child a feeling about death that is much worse than the facts would warrant. It may seem to him that the death experience cannot be managed. His vow to himself could follow the line: stay away from death and funerals. This helps explain some adult phobias of hospitals, funeral parlors, cemeteries, hearses, or the twenty-third psalm.

GRIEF AS EMPTINESS

The forces of past and present grief converge to give the loss a feeling of emptiness. When a loved one is taken, there is a craving to have his place filled. The empty chair or place at the table is a symbol. When Caesar is killed by Brutus, Shakespeare has the Romans shout, "Let Brutus be Caesar." In other words, the national leader must be replaced; the people cannot endure the emptiness of the throne or the high office. Childhood grief in the adult weeps for the father when the father of the country is fallen.

It is much easier to fill an office than it is to replace a person. There is a feeling of disloyalty in thrusting one person into the vacuum created by another. An old Arab proverb speaks to this emptiness in the spirit of the widow in saying that the

107

best time to make love to her is on the way home from the funeral. This is not an altogether ludicrous picture, because the widow's feelings tend to tell her that she must have a filling for her emptiness. It is like the pilot who has an accident and needs to fly again before his feelings withdraw too much. So the woman who loses her husband wants some quick relief for her shattered feelings. At the same time her discernment tells her that no one can take the place of her beloved. Her spirit will not allow her body to reach out so quickly to fill up the chasm. She will have to endure the pain of emptiness.

Man's haste to fill up his emptiness and to relieve his pain is the test of his character. His quick solutions through drugs, travel, or hard work can be as unreal as a romance immediately following the funeral. It is not acceptable to have the "funeral baked meats" to "furnish forth the marriage tables" (Hamlet).

It is most difficult to bear the pain of intense loss and still do nothing but wait. The waiting is a person's trust in spirit rather than in tangible things. It is the expression of trust that God has not been defeated, even though there may be no knowledge of how things will work. The waiting is the grief—and it is faith.

Jesus promised the disciples the "Spirit" or the "Comforter." The *first* ministry of the Spirit is

108

that of resolving grief. He is the comfort if men can wait. In some sense, if a person can wait he is already comforted. If there is a premature filling of this personal emptiness, there is nothing the Spirit can do; the chairs are all taken.

One of the answers for filling the loneliness is to act as though death had not occurred. This takes the shape of carrying the dead in such fashion that they are not truly given up. Thence we take on the work of the Spirit by caring for our dead (and ourselves!) in our own special make-believe way.

In other words the Spirit cannot do its work where the dead are privately reserved in the temple of the living mourner. The dead cannot be truly had or kept until they are given up. It is the power of the Spirit that helps one accept the death of his loved ones. Worded another way, this means that the dead should be put in God's hands. At least it should be admitted that they are in his hands! Where one is able to do this, he does it in the power of the Spirit.

Let us illustrate this idea from pastoral experience. The chaplain stopped by to see a woman of fifty-one facing minor surgery.

C. Miss Jones, I am Chaplain Redmond. I saw you were on the surgery list and wanted to come by to speak to you.

P. Chaplain Redmond, I'm glad to see you. They

say this surgery is not serious, but I'm worried. I have a feeling of loneliness that I've had for six years.

C. Loneliness? Could you tell me about it?

P. You see I am single. I've had this lonely feeling ever since my father died six years ago; I have felt like an orphan.

C. This was no doubt a great loss for you.

P. Yes, it was. I lived at home with my parents. My mother was an invalid for eighteen years. It was quite a struggle to take care of her and work to make a living. But I did it. It was my duty. I'm an only child.
But, Chaplain, the thing I can't seem to accept is the fact that my father died just six months after my mother died. (Tears and a great show of feeling with gestures.)

C. When you felt you could have done more for him, you lost him?

P. And more than that, I go through some strange experiences. At night when I come home, I imagine he is standing behind me when I cook supper. I close my eyes and put my hand back for him to touch me. But (with marked disappointment) he never does.

C. Miss Jones, is there any satisfying relationship with your Father in heaven as you come to face your surgery and as you work on this loss of your father?

P. I'm afraid not. I have withdrawn from the church.

C. Do you ever pray or read the Bible?

P. Not any more.

C. Let me speak a very hard truth and a very kind one. Your father is dead. You have not been able to accept it. But is there a way you can put him in the hands of God, who only raises the dead? As long as you keep him, you are responsible for him. Can you be responsible for him in the resurrection?

P. (Breathes in and out deeply.) I do have to give him up, don't I?

The prayer that followed was for her to be able to accept the painful separation that was already a fact and to affirm a God who does not die, but loves and gives blessing. Her ability to adjust to life waited on her ability to "give up" her dead; this can happen when death is no longer felt as defeat and curse.

The above case illustrates the way people get caught on the snag of grief. This turns life in a backward orientation. It attempts to freeze up the flow of time. It denies most of present reality in order to return to the past. It seeks most of all to return to the time before the great loss came.

The Spirit as Comforter is also a surgical thrust into reality. The unreal cannot be true comfort.

111

The assumption of the Spirit seems to be that man can bear what he must. It is not the task of Christianity to take away the thorns; it gives a promise of enough grace to endure. The Spirit is not a denial of death; it is a strength to bear up in the presence of emptiness—and it becomes a promise of filling.

JOB AND HIS GRIEF

The book of Job is largely a story of the management of grief.

In the first phase of his grief we see that Job had the reaction of shock, numbness, and apathy. Messengers came and told him of one calamity upon another. The Sabeans fell upon his land, seizing all his oxen and asses and killing his servants; the lightning struck, setting fire to the pastures, burning all his sheep and those tending them; the Chaldeans took all his camels in three raiding bands. Then his children were gathered in the oldest son's house having a feast when a cyclone struck, killing his seven sons and three daughters.

All this put Job in seven days of silence. During this time he sat in the dust of the ground, his body covered with boils and sores. He was deep in grief, having lost family, his possessions, and with these his status in his community. Job's wife, assuming he was under the curse of God, asked him to curse back and have done with it all.

After seven days of silent grieving Job began to speak. He began by cursing the day he was born and the night he was conceived. He regressed all the way back to birth as an attempt to get away from his unendurable pain. This is a very typical response when people have a loss that seems bigger than life itself. Hard blows turn adults back toward childhood. They make men dream of their mothers and of times long past when the world seemed young and untroubled. A man's childhood is as available in his dreams as more recent days. Small wonder that man would get away from catastrophe by escaping into the tranquillity of his early years. There was a minister who broke mentally under psychological, social, financial, and vocational pressures. In the mental hospital he took leave of the pain of it all. He would wear no clothes and would insist he was "old man Adam before sin entered the Garden." He not only returned past his sins, he went back before there was any sin anywhere. The present was so demanding and disturbing, he sought relief in the innocent past.

After theological discussions with his friends, Job takes a forward move and starts the painful journey from infancy whence he had retreated. In Chaper 29 he gets as far as the "good old days."

Oh that I were as in months past, as in the days
when God preserved me; When his candle shined
upon my head, and when by his light I walked
through darkness; as I was in the days of my
youth, when the secret of God was upon my
tabernacle; When the Almighty was yet with me,
when my children were about me; When I washed
my steps with butter, and the rock poured me
out rivers of oil. . . (Job 29:2-6 KJV)

It would be difficult to find a better description
of a man who felt he had it made. This again is
an essential part of crippling grief. A man moves
from not wanting to live at all to the point where
he can remember some past blessings and good
times. This is still not enough to get the person
to accept the present. But when this happens, the
signs are good—at least his motion is forward
instead of backward.

We see very clearly another phase that culmi-
nates in the forty-second chapter. Job's crisis is
that of becoming *present* to himself and God.
His losses are the kind that usually make it need-
ful for a person to escape into the past as a respite
from the hurt of it all. His religious argument had
been that because of his own righteousness, God
had no right to allow the happenings that crushed
him. As long as God had no such right (in Job's
eyes), there was no possibility of healing. This

meant that Job would justify himself on the ground of his sufferings. He had to hold to them as his case against an unjust order of things.

Job's three friends attempted to get him to "come clean" and confess his hidden sins. This is the only way they could preserve their theology and still account for what happened to Job. Then Elihu, with a prophetic voice, spoke, revealing the greatness and majesty of God. His approach, like all good preaching, was more to show God's grandeur than man's misery. Job's counselors had worked to get him to repent to them about his mistakes and sins. They had a method and a procedure that was supposed to get results. This is not greatly different from the revival preacher who guarantees that God will bless sinners "if you will just turn loose of that pew, walk the aisle on faith, and come forward and give me your hand."

Job's major crisis was faced squarely as he got deliverance from the past. He remarked of his former relationship to God, "I have heard of thee by the hearing of the ear; but now mine eye seeth thee" (Job 42:5 KJV).

When a man is present to God he goes through a crisis in his self-awareness. Job continued his words saying, "Wherefore I abhor myself, and repent in dust and ashes" (42:6). His repentance

115

was not toward the preacher or the congregation on the third stanza of the invitation hymn. It was in real life in an earth-shaking view of himself before God.

All the preaching of Job's counselors failed. They sought to break Job's defenses down and expose his nakedness. This only drove Job into his own defense. So it usually goes when preaching (or counseling) becomes openly judgmental. When the finger is pointed at a man, his defenses usually go up whether he is innocent or guilty. If Job had been a very dependent person, he could have followed the prescribed method of making atonement and confession. Then he could have spent the rest of his years with his "boils" infesting the lining of his stomach or intestines. He could not have "had it out" with God as he did. He had feelings that other men hoped he would squelch. Before God he was able to surrender his case because he could surrender himself.

Job's posture up to the encounter with God was a stance of looking to the past. But to see God is esssentially to be in the present. This is the action of the Spirit. This is God's power to move a man along the path of reality.

No doubt the action of the Spirit is that of giving a man "everything double," as was the case with Job. When Job could surrender his past,

116

he could actually have it. In reality the past is always available because every detail of it is recorded in the feeling life. But the person who cannot give it up will find himself in bondage to it. If a man can yield it to God, that man will no longer need to plead or defend his case. It took a powerful vision of God for Job to give up his hold on the past and the hold the past had on him.

Jesus said a man would have to surrender his life in order to have it. This can easily apply to the past. The crisis in the lives of the apostles was similar to that in Job's life. In both cases there is a problem of a pleasant past coming to a halt in a sudden blow. In neither case could the men come up with a desire to go on living. When the meaning of life is gone, men usually respond with a will to stop the whole affair. Unless they come to meaning and renewal in the face of great crisis, they begin a process of withdrawal and resignation.

Perhaps none of the apostles felt that life could ever get off the snag after the crucifixion of Jesus. Not even the Resurrection had power to deliver them from their regression. Only in the coming of the Spirit did they get "everything double." They got a new image of their own usefulness in the ongoing purposes of God. They were able to give up their lives lived in Jesus' presence in order

117

to take hold of his promise of "greater works." Their choice was to live in the past—a most glorious past—or come to terms with themselves in a present that was devoid of the most magnetic personality they had even encountered.

But life could not go on without Jesus. They had him in such a way that they could not get him out of their systems. Still they had to give up Jesus "after the flesh." They could not know the meaning of his life with them until they entered life in the Spirit. The same could be spoken of Job. When he encountered God he did not get his children back any more than the apostles got Jesus back. In his encounter, he was able to accept what he had already lost. In the economy of the Spirit nothing is lost. So what Job lost he was able to keep—he had his past put in a relationship that preserved the meaning.

In dealing with grief, we come to see the meaning of giving life up and getting it back. As long as a person holds to his beloved who has died, he holds himself against all spiritual blessing.

EVERY MAN'S GRIEF

The apostle who held to "Jesus after the flesh" was doing the same thing Job did in holding to and living in his past. The *memory* of the past is not enough to sustain. This even tends to en-

118

slave more because it actually judges God as being incapable of doing as well in the future as he has already done. The essence of despair is in putting God in the past tense.

The spiritual solution to grief comes in getting one's feelings back into relationship after great personal loss. There it also depends on one hearing and accepting the tolling of the bell for him as well as all the others who must hear and heed the call. Unless the death of a loved one speaks of my own death, then I do not hear an essential part of the message.

In a real sense, one man grieves for another man according to the degree of closeness of kinship or friendship. But there must be a power outside the one in grief to help him come to terms with intolerable loss. He can in the Spirit find solution to loss without getting lost in despair. This was Job's route until he was convinced he still had a future in God and that God had a future for him. This can best be accomplished if the dead, held in great reverence, can be reverently acknowledged to be in God's care and keeping.

It may sound rather strange to insist on the living giving their dead into God's hands, but this holding on in subtle forms is psychologically explosive. For example, a chaplain visited a woman who was scheduled for minor surgery. In a few

119

minutes it became obvious that she was in grief. She went on to explain how she had lost her oldest son two years before in a motorcycle accident. She wept and said she had not been able to give him up. She remarked that her grief was just as fresh as it was at first. The chaplain, seeing the danger signals asked her where she felt her son was. (He was not asking a theological question about his afterlife.) As quick as a flash, she checked his eyes to see if he understood her feelings. Then she reached her hand out beside the bed, as if patting her son on the head, saying, "He's right here beside me. He's been there all along."

After long discussion and several visits later, this woman realized she had to get out of the past, give up her dead son, and come to terms with reality. She had six children who needed her; yet she had difficulty accepting what had to be done to get on with the task of life. She felt an inner sense of disloyalty at putting this chosen son out of the center of her life. But she was able to establish a new sense of commitment in God that freed her from any of the deep resolves she had made for her firstborn son. She had to realize, like Job, that one's commitments to God are deeper. This realization comes about when a person faces the deep conflict between going back and going on.

Good spiritual care does not force a person along the forward path in grief. This is a step that a person must take as he is able. The trained pastor will remain alert in all grief situations. He has a right to ask a widow if she has gone through the pain of her loss. She will know immediately whether she has skirted around the deeper part. With patience and skill she can be led back to the point of her departure from reality. The spirit within her hungers for the correct solution to such problems. She may not know how to avoid the tendency to escape into fantasy. She may need to talk about how far and in what ways she does this. These things can usually be given up when they can be shared.

This is another way of saying that reality with its pains is more rewarding than fantasy. The characters in fantasy cannot finally relate and give love. One cannot fantasize human relations without doing the same to the God relation. In these situations it becomes the major responsibility of the spiritual person to represent reality. We stress again that men can do what they must to come to terms with the real world and real relationships. The pastor who allows respite from reality in helping people play games may not be fully aware of what their greater needs are.

The curse of grief can be removed, or at least it can be borne, when there is the assurance that its power is not too great for God's blessings to prevail.

GRIEF IN THE LIFE OF JESUS

No doubt Jesus dealt with grief in his own life and ministry. The place where he came into direct struggle with death was following his baptism. It was at this point that he had to commit himself to the road that lead with certainty to Calvary and the cross. The temptations in the wilderness were in some sense his attempting to fashion a program that would accomplish his goal and at the same time save his life or at least avoid the ultimate nakedness and humiliation. He apparently decided very firmly and resolutely that there was no way to be "Messiah" as Israel had dreamed for a thousand years and he perhaps had hoped up until this time.

In the wilderness experience of the temptations he shook off all the longed-for alternatives and entered into the grief of having to die. When he fixed his course and withstood all the options that might have spared his life, Luke tells us, "And Jesus returned in the power of the Spirit into Galilee" (Luke 4:14).

Could it be that Jesus, in this experience of his own death, unlocked the mysterious cycle or movement of the Spirit? Perhaps it took forty days of fasting, searching, waiting, and dying in order to find the necessary renewal that was the Spirit. The Gospel accounts relate that the Spirit was

122

present in the baptism. But is the presence of the Spirit different after the wilderness in that this presence in some sense is no longer external but the very inner life of Jesus? Is the Spirit the replacement of the "kingdom of Israel," which was a kind of death for him to have to surrender? The Spirit was his Comforter.

At any rate, it is from this "dying" in the wilderness that Jesus moved with power and authority to work, not for the kingdom of Israel, but for the kingdom of God. He moved to call his disciples and to enter actively into his plan and program that would terminate some three years later in his death.

A case can be made for the idea that Jesus prepared his disciples for his own wilderness experience so that they could also enter the life of the Spirit or so that the Spirit could enter their lives. This was accomplished in his own death and the final destruction of their hope for a Messiah that would "restore the kingdom to Israel" (Acts 1:6). It is not likely that they could fully enter their grief and loss until they were forced to give up these hopes. And it was at this point that they could wait. They were no doubt made empty and sorrowful; Pentecost became their filling.

No man today can repeat the grief that the disciples had. He will have his own grief in his own way. No man will have the same temptations as

Jesus had, yet each must face his own temptations. But in some sense grief and temptation are the same. Our temptation is to deal with our loss and emptiness without going through the intolerable cycle of waiting. We tend to take the initiative away from the Spirit, and we miss out on our own private Pentecost. We, in our anxiety, tend to find our own ways of filling the void. One man said, after the loss of his wife of twenty-three years, "I just couldn't stand it any longer, so I took a trip to Europe."

Grief can lead man into a wilderness of temptation where he will come to know that he cannot have his own little kingdom of hopes. What he loved most, he will have to surrender. Perhaps what he could not live without is now taken away. Of course he can hold out for a magical or fantastic solution. Where he does this his grief will rob him of any further growth. He will remain in the wilderness no matter what he does to change the situation.

So it is in life—many people can date their grief crisis as their break from reality and growth. One father could not accept that his beloved oldest daughter got pregnant out of wedlock. From that time his health gave way with a whole series of physical maladies—stomach ulcer, heart palpitations, loss of weight. In not being able to face

124

it he retreated behind hard work, excessive use of tranquilizers, frequent travel, and alcohol.

The ability to wait might be the chief Christian virtue. The creative power of God promises to be at work in our waiting. Man's despair is his giving up on God's ability to do any new thing, or it is his unwillingness to have the course of his life take a new shape. The curse of grief speaks loudly in the life that must hold on to what it wanted and could never have. The blessing is promised to the one who can still expectantly wait for new life that comes out of his own dying.

VI

The Vows of Childhood Revamped

The man who feels obliged to carry out his vows from childhood can become a prisoner of his own past. Maturity is the ability to "put away childish things" in such a way that one is no longer compelled to wear the ill-fitting garments of earlier days. Yet one does not easily and openly shake off these vows as though they were loosely worn and quickly shed. They are as much a part of any adult as his thoughts and dreams. They are interwoven with the fabric of his being, and they do much to color his attitudes and behavior.

There is no church or public ceremony that gives release or freedom from vows once spoken in the most secret chambers of the inner self. In fact there is little recognition that many people wait for deliverance from the prison house of the childhood (or immature) vow. If one cannot get release on one hand and cannot keep the vows on the other, he is unable to go forward. For example, a woman twenty-three years of age could not move toward the men she dated with affection and seriousness. She wore a ring on each hand that her brother had given her at different times. Before she could be free to make progress toward the marriage vow, she had to deal with what the rings meant to her. They kept her "true" to her feelings developed toward her brother when they slept together in the same sleeping bag as children on long summer camping trips. The brother was some four years older and unmarried. When this woman took her rings off and was able to enter into serious courtship and marriage, her brother did the same. He married five months after the sister married. In each case there was the kind of commitment that children make in all innocence; but the commitment needed release, and the release came as these hidden vows could float to the surface of recognition.

There tends to be a general feeling that God binds us to all vows made in secret. In fact we tend to make him witness to them in the assumption that they must be kept at all cost. It is as

127

though God could not take into account the changes of time and circumstance that may call for a change in the vows.

VOWS TAKEN ON PAIN OF CURSE

The soldier under fire in combat takes a vow to be a preacher if he is spared. The man in critical injury promises to "do what God wants" if he can get well. The woman vows to give her child to God if he will remove the curse of barrenness. There is usually a curse spoken with such vows: "Let me be accursed if I fail to do this." For example, the psalmist speaks to the nature of the vow made with a curse:

> If I forget you, O Jerusalem,
>   let my right hand wither!
> Let my tongue cleave to the roof
>   of my mouth,
> if I do not remember you,
> if I do not set Jerusalem
>   above my highest joy!
>   (Psalm 137:5-6)

The sworn oaths to faithfulness are usually done in all solemnity and sacredness before God. They cannot be ignored or taken lightly once the crisis is gone. They must be dealt with as very powerful realities. It is at this point that some

128

people start to live under a self-imposed curse because they fail to perform the promises and vows made under stress or fear.

Spiritual reality says that God does not bind us to vows made in critical circumstances so much as we bind ourselves. This tends to produce guilt that must be resolved. This is acknowledged in the law: "'If any one utters with his lips a rash oath to do evil or to do good, any sort of rash oath that men swear, and it is hidden from him [if he forgets it], when he comes to know it he shall in any of these be guilty" (Leviticus 5:4). Jesus realized this tendency to swear oneself in a binding way and judged it to be out of character with mature spirituality. He said we were not to swear by heaven, by the earth, by Jerusalem, or by our own head, adding, "Let what you say be simply 'Yes' or 'No'; anything more than this comes from evil" (Matthew 5:37).

In saying the above, Jesus seems to be releasing man from oaths sworn "unto the Lord." These are the vows once spoken to get us off the hook, but that tend to place us under the self-imposed curse. The integrity of the spirit will not allow a person to treat these vows lightly in shunning them, ignoring them, or even forgetting them. They will go on producing guilt until they are freely forgiven—not necessarily paid up. There too, the entire picture is changed when we come

129

to accept the fact that God can and will release us from the accursed vow, and does not intend that we bind ourselves by these things.

We have been speaking of vows made in a more adult frame of reference. Let them symbolize the deeper and more powerful (often hidden) ones that children take. A man of fifty fell into deep depression of spirit following the death of his mother. He was the eldest of three children and had lost his father at age ten. He was the chief help in caring for his mother and his younger brother and sister. He said he promised himself two things before God: "If he would help me, I would never be hungry again, and I would always take care of my mother." At the time of his problem he was very wealthy in land, cattle, timber, and oil. But much of his reason for existing was now gone in the loss of his mother. His vow had not taken into account the fact that he would not *always* have his mother, and it forgot that the solution to all problems did not come in "houses and lands." It was not easy for this man to get free from the ten-year-old boy who had dominated his behavior. He had so taken his father's place that he was failing to be a father and husband. He came to say he was "twenty years late" realizing his true adult responsibilities. He was then able to recommit his energies and resources to his wife and children, who had a more rightful claim upon them. He had bound and virtually imprisoned his spirit by what he had determined to do in childhood.

The vow creates spiritual poverty because it puts the child in control of the man; at least the less mature self becomes owner or guard over the more mature. It tends to replace God with one's own resolve. In effect it tends to say to God, "Help me out of this situation, and a curse be upon me if I ever let it happen again." It also has the undertone of, "God help me this time, and I won't bother you again." In a subtle way it promises to repay God with interest for all his trouble. Still another hidden assumption is that God brings on the crisis in order to get man's attention, his works, or his tithe, and, of course, his promises.

Behind the immature vow goes the image of God as tyrant rather than Father. This puts a person in the position of having to appease God rather than to relate in love and dependent trust. The vow sworn to God as tyrant can only be repaid out of a sense of duty and compulsion. Such a vow can become a shield or defense between the self and God. It assumes that God is a taskmaster who demands full payment going all the way back to every utterance or suggestion of a promise. It is the nature of man to try to rid himself of the burden of his own making; he comes to exact a performance of himself that is beyond his ability. He assumes that once he pays all his vows he will have a clean account and freedom from God's exacting hand. No person tends to work knowingly to get "free" from God, yet without being aware of it we struggle to get into a position of not having to depend on him so much or wait for him in patience.

THE MARRIAGE VOWS

The vows taken at the altar between a man and a woman speak to the revamping of childhood vows: "Forsaking all others"—this is a freeing personally and even legally of promises made under less mature circumstances. Few lovers come to marriage without some past experiences of commitment. "When the blood burns, how prodigal the soul lends the tongue vows" (Hamlet, Act I, Sc. 3). Whose blood does not burn with the vows and promises even of puppy love? All these are cleared up as two lovers pledge themselves in faithfulness and affection. The father "gives the bride away" as an act of surrendering the claims of the childhood family. The girl has now become a woman and is not bound by the many vows and promises made in secret to look after or take care of her parents. If she keeps such vows they still must be second in importance to the vows made to her husband. The same freeing is declared for the man: "For this cause shall a man leave his father and mother." He cannot leave them if he holds secret reservations that go back to his own childhood past.

To be sure, many of the childhood resolves do not immediately give way in marriage. We have already indicated that many of them cannot be remembered. Yet as they come to light, they are no longer binding—at least their grip is weaker if the marriage vows can be seen for what they really are.

Many stories of shipwrecked marriages go back to vows spoken on top of older childhood vows that did not lose their grip and hold of the past. Many wedding rings are forced on top of imaginary rings that continue to say, "My heart belongs to daddy." A college-age daughter signed her letter to her father: "To the man first in my life now and always." The wise father responded with appreciation for his daughter's voicing of her love, but said, "While I appreciate your love, I will not bind you to any vows that are 'always'." There are many fathers who are hurt or outraged when their daughters dare move out of the childhood pattern of father loyalty. These fathers do not give their daughters away except with crossed fingers.

What is true of daughters may be even more true of sons. We do not subject mothers to the act of giving their sons away. It could be a very healthy thing—a double parent ceremony! Few men come to the altar without a recollection of the tenderness and care of their mothers. Most of them have, as little boys, told their mothers how they would "be your daddy" if they would not cry or if they would not worry.

VOWS AND VOCATION

Adults need to be free to choose their life's work. To be sure there are many such choices made by persons in childhood, and many times this works well enough. For the most part, an early choice has some liability. The child is not often wise enough to give due and full consideration to the vocation or calling best suited for him.

If, because of a childhood vow growing out of a crisis, a person feels that he must enter a calling to protect the vow, he is not entering by free choice but is under obligation. If he makes his choice in this fashion, he may only be responding to his fears of being labeled a spiritual draft-dodger. If one enters a vocation to pay a debt, please a parent, or stave off a curse, he just might

134

suffer for lack of motivation for his task. The more he is under compulsion to do a certain work, the less likely he is to get enjoyment from it. Vocational choice should not be determined by a parent's feelings and wishes. This is not to say the attitudes of others are unimportant; it is only to say that one's own demands upon himself are more important. One is not free to choose if he must please others first, and he is not free if he is under compulsion to prove something.

THE VOW AND CHRISTIAN MATURITY

Christianity does not set one free from all commitments, resolves, and vows of the past. Yet there is a need to distinguish between the ones of these that are binding and the ones that are not.

Something of a guideline can be set in saying that responsibilities hold where obligations have been made to other people. For example, a person in becoming a free and mature Christian is not free to divorce his wife if she fails to take the same step. Debts remain the same. In fact, the Christian will take care of debts where only his word was given; these should stand as his bond. If he has promised his word to anyone or any group to do anything that he holds to be out of character with his growth, he will need to voice his reasons for

135

changing his course of behavior. Even the prisoner who is converted will have to make his prison his area of service to God. The adult who cannot get free from an open commitment made to the church in his teens may need to talk this all out with his pastor.

If one has promised himself before God to do or not do a certain thing, this promise can be reviewed freely as one comes to understand that God is no longer a demanding tyrant. The entire picture changes with the Christian image of God as caring Father.

A certain man became a Christian ten years after his war experience. He had a problem of having taken an expensive piece of jewelry from a German home. He did not even so much as remember the town where he had done this, much less the particular home. He felt he should do something about it, but he could not find a solution. He tried to resolve it all by saying nothing could be done. He felt he had more right to it than anyone else, and it was impossible to restore it to its rightful owner. He had to be faced with the fact that he could not keep the jewelry and still find peace and forgiveness. He had to do what he could to make restoration. He found some peace in selling the jewelry and giving the proceeds to his church. He had secretly hoped that in becoming a Christian he would be forgiven in such a way that he could forget about the jewelry. It would not be forgotten; it had to be offered up in order to remove a cancerous mass in his spirit.

Christianity is not a reprieve upon the past. It makes us responsible for all we have done, and it calls upon us to set things right as much as we are able. On the other hand, the vows we have taken silently and privately before God need to be reviewed and considered seriously. In becoming a Christian one stands like a bridgegroom at the altar who has come to commit himself to his bride all the days of his life. Christianity expects new commitments on top of old commitments; it expects new vows to replace the old ones, new goals and purposes to phase out the less important ones.

There is a great difference between paying a vow and realizing that one has vowed amiss. If one promised God what one cannot do, God will be the first to release him, if he can release himself. Where a man holds himself to a past vow he cannot perform, he actually seals off further spiritual growth. He makes it seem that God is holding him to an impossible commitment. This also stops spiritual development. It seems to prove God wrong; it makes a case for the wounded self and tends to justify a withdrawal from life and growth.

137

THE VOW AND THE PAIN OF GROWTH

A woman of thirty-five said she had given up, there was no need to try any more. Life was simply not worth the effort. She was in despair. She explained that the shattering blow came when she discovered a liquor bottle hidden in the closet. It told her that her husband was an alcoholic. Her response was, "Oh God, not *again.*" She explained that her father had been an alcoholic, and she had promised herself in a childhood vow that she would never live in marriage with an alcoholic man. Now it was upon her in full force. She was rather regular in her attendance at worship and said she prayed often, but seemed to get very little out of it. When asked what God was like as she approached him she said, "He seems to be looking down at me with just a bit of a sneer." To her it seemed that God was intent on trapping her, and now he had her! She had responded to her agony by setting about fully to destroy her husband. She accomplished it in two ways— first, by going on a spending spree and building up a big debt, and, second, by saying the most brutal things about him to all their friends and neighbors.

This woman had the touch of a sneer on her face, and it was obvious she had made God in her own image. In her compulsive and driving

138

desire to get away from and above her childhood home, she had only helped bring it into being. It was a long and slow process, but a very rewarding one, to help her develop an image of God as Father in such a way that Father was not her alcoholic father or husband. As this happened she was able to start building a better image of her husband to their friends. As soon as she showed the slightest concern for her husband's needs he joined Alcoholics Anonymous and at the same time greatly improved his financial position to take care of her debts. This told her in a strong way that he really cared. This began to reinforce the fact of God's care.

Many people simply become emotional dropouts at the point in adult life where they have to face again the painful hurt of earlier years. They suffer once more the very hurt they resolved they would never have again. The more they build up protection against such pain, the more they are likely to be caught in it from some blind side. Many of them are simply unable to cope with such terror or fear, and they can only retreat. They must have someone who can understand enough to help them through it. In the above case, the woman came for help some two years after her crushing experience. That was very late because of the many things she did destructively during that time.

People can do what they must, but they are

more likely to do it if they do not have to do it *alone*. Any caring person must take the responsibility to help them face what they must do, or at least stay with them until they can start the forward motion of life so as to go *through* their troubled areas.

VII

The Blessing as Healing

Whoever brings acceptance in a total way brings healing. Whoever cannot accept affirmation from another cannot be healed. Whoever shuts himself off from sharing his deeper self imposes on himself a kind of isolation or banishment from healing. In seeking to work things out "by himself" one can only revolve from self-hate to self-pity and back again. There is no way out of the cycle. A genuine self-acceptance must be started at some point outside the self; it must come from another self who has been able in turn to accept healing from his own brokenness. The other and outside person cannot intrude or force himself into the picture. He must be authorized or given power by the broken one to accept and heal. He does not hold the authority within himself; it must be granted or permitted by the one in need, and it must be asked for or sought.

THE POWER OF BLESSING

Just as one life comes from another life, so blessing comes from another. When Abraham blessed Isaac, he passed his life to Isaac in a special way; the potency of the father was given to the son. The blessing in this sense was a willing away of the father on behalf of the son, it was a dying for another to live.

In turn Isaac blessed Jacob in bestowing his being and existence upon Jacob. Then the twin brother Esau turned with the plaintive cry, "Have you not reserved a blessing for me?" (Genesis 27: 36). But Isaac had given his substance to Jacob, and there was no turning back. The remnant of a blessing was taken only as a kind of curse, and Esau took a vow to kill his brother Jacob.

While the picture is seldom that strong on the modern scene, it still points up the problem of family favoritism. The following retells the ancient story.

Ernest B., a man of forty-six, came saying he could not understand his nagging depression that had lasted for about a year. During that time he said he had begun to "curse like a sailor," a thing he had never done before. He said he was reared in a small town where his father operated a cane mill. He related how he detested the foul language around the mill, and he added, "My father was the worst of them all." His mother saw that Ernest went to church regularly, and this reinforced his resolve never to swear as the others around him did. For a time he had seriously considered going into the ministry. He went on to tell how he had struggled to make his father take notice of his religion and his serious efforts to make good grades. Ernest had a younger brother who was a good athlete. This claimed the father's attention so much that he "never missed a game," but at the same time there seemed to be nothing Ernest could do even to please his father. He related how this pattern had continued through the years, with the father's attention and thoughts going to his brother's children. The father died eighteen months before Ernest came for help. When asked about whether he had been able to squarely face his father's death, he said, "There were plenty of tears, but I couldn't find the time or place to let go." He said his wife reminded him often that he had turned upon his only son with his curses; this was straining his marriage. He wondered if he should not give up his Sunday school class because he was such an "unfit father and husband." He said matters were made much worse when his wife turned to his brother for advice. He moved to another room in the house and "lost all desire for her."

It was obvious that Ernest had taken his own father's place. He had not been able to turn loose a father who had not shown him love and care. As he came to face his grief in the outpouring torrent of sorrow and crying, he began the slow process of healing in coming to his own life and usefulness. He accepted that the blessing of God was not denied to him simply because his father was impotent to bless him. He kept his Sunday school class as a way of finding his own opportunity to minister to others. As he found blessing he felt he could give it. His thoughts about a possible divorce were given up, and he was able to move back to his bedroom with his wife.

The blessing is the only thing stronger than a "blessing out" or a curse. In the case of Ernest there had been the constant love of his mother, but that was not enough. The blessing is more than love—it is the very renewal of life itself, it is the power to beget. Such power cannot be "nurtured" into existence; nurture is the power of the woman. It must be "spoken" into being by the authority of the Father or by the one who speaks for him; it is in a profound sense the power

144

to heal, to make alive. In a Christian sense it is the power to re-beget, or a begetting to a second birth.

The blessing is a freeing power. A man with four sons centered his interst and concern upon one of them. When he came to die, the blessing child lived two thousand miles from home. The other three sons were clustered round him in apartments on the same block. The Prodigal Son could take his part of the inheritance and go. There is truth in the saying, "Bless me and let me go." The unblessed child tends to make many false starts. He goes out but he returns, he leaves home but he cannot stay. If he does stay, his dreams remain in his father's house.

The blessing child is the child of grace, he does not have to prove himself. Sometimes, like the Prodigal Son, his conduct is the worst, but he can still look at himself without despair. The blessing is there to affirm to him that there is hope for his healing. The unblessed son, like the Elder Brother, tends to base his hope on his own good behavior; this is not enough to sustain him, at least it does not free him to be. He has difficulty facing his own brokenness and his need for healing. His good conduct becomes his own proof against his reaching out for help. He is a child of works, and he places himself under what the Apostle Paul

145

calls the "curse of the law." His own perfectionistic strivings keep him from ever reaching his ideal.

THE GOOD NEWS AS HEALING POWER

The easy solution is for every family to make each child a grace child. But parents are simply not able to do this; they come to parenthood out of a set of experiences that are already shaping their responses. They will pass these on with faithful repetition to future generations. There must be an outside interruption that becomes both a disturbing and freeing power. This power stops the son from being enslaved to the absent blessing and from waiting around until the father dies so he can get it: "Let me first bury my father."

The Good News is the word of God to Abraham—"Get thee out of thy father's house"—and it is the word to the disciples—"Leave your father and mother." The past cannot be resolved on the scene; it must be put behind in geography, so it can be put behind in time. If it can be left it can be possessed; if it is kept it possesses us. One of the greatest sorrows in life comes at the point of breaking with all the childhood past. It can create as much anxiety as any experience. One can never get enough to fill up his longing, but one can never have it without leaving it. The fol-

146

lowing story will illustrate much of what I am saying.

George K. was a high school senior, a straight A student, and a star athlete. He came for help because of a constant anxiety over feelings that he might die. In his fear every headache was a brain tumor, every stomachache a cancer, and every chest pain a heart attack. In addition to this, every siren was an air raid, every fire alarm was his home burning, and military service was certain death. His usual habit was that of studying until eleven o'clock in the evening and then dashing through the house for an hour or so calling on his parents to comfort him in his panic about death. He had been to a psychiatrist two years before for the same fears. He said this went back to early grammar school when he developed panic at school for fear that he would get home and find that his parents and older brother had moved away and left him.

George could not get the assurance he needed from his parents, and he constantly called on them to the point of their exasperation. Their attention took the form of holding him, massaging his back, talking to him, and trying to reassure him. He demanded much physical closeness to get to sleep. Some nights he would wake up and demand more.

George was not only a leader in school, he was outstanding in the life of his church and was considering entering the ministry. However, his church activities were becoming difficult, and sermons always made him feel he was for some reason under a spell of doom—in other words, God would give him curse rather than blessing. He was in great conflict about sex, especially the feelings and the fantasies he entertained about his dates. He felt God wanted something from him and would not accept him unless he did or gave what God demanded. His praying was mostly an exercise in trying to get God to initiate something about what he wanted. This always ended in frustration. He also asked God to solve his questions about death. When asked to explain this he told of how he wanted his dead grandfather to come back quietly and tell him everything was all right; then he would be able to accept death. As he pondered this solution, he realized he could not have such an experience and be able to tell anybody else about it. So this was also impossible as a solution.

In the home settings, George first said he and his brother were treated alike in every way. The brother was in college. The more he thought about it, the more he felt his brother got his mother's major attention. On the other hand, he came to realize his father was unable to move toward him because the mother blocked it. She was much stronger than the father and directed family activity as well as finances with a firm hand. In coming to know his parents as people he accepted their frailties and mortality. As he faced these facts he could begin to deal more comfortably with his own mortal nature. These discussions would be disturbed with such a reminder as "this is proof that George is going to die." We came repeatedly back to the middle of the panic until he could live comfortably with it.

In the beginning of his visits George described the Christ event in his own thinking as a drama acted out for our sake to give us comfort with the story of the Resurrection. But he got no comfort out of it. It was shattering for him to think that Jesus died in faith and trust rather than in certain knowledge about Easter and the Resurrection. As he absorbed the truth of it he said, "I've been asking God to do for me what he didn't do for Jesus Christ!" He realized he had been trying to be an exception in an impossible way. This led rather naturally to his thinking he had to die for his own unacceptable feelings and imaginations. He was able to give up the necessity of his own death as his personal salvation. As he could do this, Christianity began to be a healing force. He could begin to think of separation from his parents, of college, and even the draft. The deep sense of curse and alienation from his inner self began to give way as he found the more powerful

149

affirmation in the gospel of God's love and blessing. He did not have to get the blessing in an
earthly sense from his father, who could not really
reach out to him more than to rub his back.

ORDINATION, BLESSING, AND HEALING

As in the case of George K., there needs to be a
"laying on of hands" in growth and nurture, else
the child will have difficulty giving up the hands
that have served his growing needs. The parents
pass their lives to their children in the many ser-
vices of their hands. Where the hand serves with
reluctance it does not fulfill its purpose in the life
of the child. A halfhearted service is crippling.

Jesus called, trained, and set aside (ordained)
the apostles for the service of others. (The word
"service" literally means "therapy.") One cannot
separate service from healing, nor can one separate
healing from blessing. There was no healing in
ancient medicine or religion apart from the laying
on of hands. The life of the healer was the best
medicine for the sick. In placing hands on the
sick, the healer gave the world's most primitive
form of transfusion or infusion. In this kindly act
the healer gave himself.

In more sophisticated and technological times
the healer tends to lean more heavily on the laboratory and pharmacology. No modern man would

want to be without these benefits. But man has not climbed above his dependent need to look to the healer as the one with blessing. For example, the doctor cannot prevent cancer. He can treat it, and often he finds respite or even cure. Yet the one suffering from cancer tends to *feel* as though it were a crystallizing of the primitive power of curse. It may be as important to help with the feelings about cancer (and curse) as it is to try to bring healing to the body. At this time the doctor's hands can tell the patient that there is still contact with life. He does not have to be shut off from the living world before the time of death. Yet where the healer withdraws behind his methods and techniques to protect himself from a feeling of pain or failure, he misses some of his greatest opportunities to serve.

The Christian is a healer of broken spirits. He will need to "gird up his loins" and be willing to lay his hands gently, yet perhaps firmly, on the tender areas of suffering, so that he might give the very strength of his life in sharing his blessing with others.

THE SHAPE OF THE BLESSING

The following is something of an adaptation that could add some light to the blessing promised in the beatitudes.

151

The blessing is for the poor in spirit: theirs is the kingdom of heaven.

The blessing is for the grief stricken: they shall find comfort.

The blessing is for the meek: they shall inherit the earth.

The blessing is for those who hunger and thirst for goodness: they shall be satisfied.

The blessing is for those who show mercy: they will obtain mercy.

The blessing is for those whose hearts are single: they will see God.

The blessing is for the peacemakers: they shall be called sons of God.

The blessing is for those who get into trouble for doing right: theirs is the kingdom of heaven.

Yon have the blessing if when men curse you, you do not curse back.

THE POWER TO BLESS

The intent of the gospel is to bring the blessing of Abraham to more than one child. The son of love by the wife of love tends to be the blessing child. Shakespeare is a master at showing how the bastard child, being a child of curse, brings trouble and curse to all around him (King Lear). Ira Levin, in *Rosemary's Baby*, shows how the curse produces a monster. He also indicates at the

152

close of his novel that love and blessing start the slow process of transformation of the monster child into a person.

The gospel is the courage to take blessing to all the Esaus who suffer "without the camp." It asserts power over all the demonic forces of curse and has the courage to include the leper, the demonic, and Zacchaeus. It extends the umbrella of God's loving care to all men everywhere and to each particular man at his point of need.

As long as we can point to the "monster" in the other person, we delay the day when we have to deal with him in ourselves. Jesus had the fortitude to identify with every accursed person and the accursed part of each person. He discouraged the tendency we have to isolate and banish our inner demons of fear, anxiety, and guilt. He knew they would only consume our spiritual vitality, leaving us a prey to hate, discord, division, and sickness. He said, "Love your enemies," and he knew the "enemy" was pictured in the person who mirrored the demon that troubled us most.

We have all come through the primitive fears in our childhood existence. No one can escape the various aspects of some curse upon feelings; these include sex, anger, death, or even love. These feelings of curse are increased where there is illegitimacy, minority status, prolonged disease, deformity, poverty, grief, or extreme ridicule. Adults

153

tend to play children's games when they isolate the black man, shun the leper, laugh at the hunchback or the retarded, slander the poor, and ridicule the mentally ill. They are only trying to relieve their self-rejection by rejecting outwardly.

The Christ-spirit does not reserve the blessing for the intelligent, the affluent, the white, the fortunate, the healthy, the wise, and the productive. It is really no respecter of race, religion, rank, power, past achievement, or personal piety.

Our "salvation" or our healing does not come in our strivings to rise above what we are or what other men are. Our own ladders by which we climb are only an attempt to disown the shameful or unacceptable side of the self. To be sure, we can look at our starched shirts and our bank accounts and feel a temporary pride in not being like men in the ghetto, the mental hospital, or the prison.

In a most convincing way, Jesus made common cause with the prisoner, the sick, the demon-possessed, the widow, the fatherless, and the "sinner." His family and friends worried about the company he kept. But he had to feel the curse of these people in order to make his acceptance a reality, a blessing. He could do it because these people were no threat to his own wholeness—he did not seem to have to prove anything or to defend anything. He would not draw a line between "good"

154

and "bad," between "rich" and "poor," Jew and Greek, black and white.

In some sense, then, the cross is a pushing of all men into a great commonality. None can claim blessing for himself in his own right. Blessing does not come from good works or great heritage. Yet no man wants to start from nothing. The pious man resents being leveled with the prostitute, and the rich protests being the brother of the poor. The cross will not let us live in peace and wholeness unless we affirm there that we are brother to all the broken ones. It is there that Cain and Abel, Jacob and Esau, the Prodigal Son and Elder Brother discover that the Father's desire is to give blessing to all his children alike. Human salvation is usually based on some factor of personal worth or special merit. The cross sets off the rage of the human race because all special claims are done away with, and the origin and power of all healing and blessing begins with God, who sees and knows us as we are.

Index